BARTHES

A BEGINNER'S GUIDE

MIREILLE RIBIÈRE

Hodder & Stoughton

A MEMBER OF THE HODDER HEADLINE GROUP

Orders: please contact Bookpoint Ltd, 130 Milton Park, Abingdon, Oxon OX14 4SB. Telephone: (44) 01235 827720, Fax: (44) 01235 400454. Lines are open from 9.00–6.00, Monday to Saturday, with a 24-hour message answering service. Email address: orders@bookpoint.co.uk

British Library Cataloguing in Publication Data
A catalogue record for this title is available from The British Library

ISBN 0 340 84499 X

First published 2002
Impression number   10 9 8 7 6 5 4 3 2 1
Year 2007 2006 2005 2004 2003 2002

Cover photo from Popperfoto.
Typeset by Transet Limited, Coventry, England.
Printed in Great Britain for Hodder & Stoughton Educational, a division of Hodder Headline Plc, 338 Euston Road, London NW1 3BH by Cox & Wyman, Reading, Berks.

BARTHES

A BEGINNER'S GUIDE

CONTENTS

DEDICATION
For Tim

ACKNOWLEDGEMENTS

I wish to thank Jan Baetens and Charlie Mansfield for their comments on the manuscript. I am also grateful to the publishing team at Hodder and Stoughton, notably Mel Thompson and Helen Hart who initiated and oversaw the project.

Barthes in perspective

Roland Barthes (1915–1980) was probably the most important French thinker to emerge from the post-war period. He was part of every major intellectual movement in the humanities that came out of Metropolitan France between 1945 and 1980 and he became a figure of international repute. At a time of great social, political and intellectual change, Barthes represented an unconventional, yet often rigorous, way of thinking which had considerable appeal.

Unlike many influential figures in the history of ideas, Barthes did not make a ground-breaking intellectual discovery which he then proceeded to refine and expand. From the start, Barthes borrowed elements from theories developed by others. He combined and used these elements to build his own original theories and having achieved recognition for his endeavours, he would simply move on. As he successively distanced himself from what he had initially expounded, he proceeded to offer new ways of looking at things. The result is a multifaceted body of work in which successive generations have found interest and intellectual stimulation.

Roland Barthes was born on 12 November 1915 in Cherbourg into a middle-class family. He was barely one year old when his father, a naval officer, died in combat. His mother then moved to Bayonne, a coastal town in southwestern France, where Roland spent a happy, if lonely, childhood. In 1924, they moved to Paris. Barthes started his secondary education and made good academic progress, while his mother earned a meagre living as a bookbinder.

At the beginning of 1934, the future looked promising: Barthes would take his *baccalauréat* that year, prepare for the entrance exams to the prestigious École Normale Supérieure and then become a teacher. It was not to be. In May 1934, he suffered his first attack of pulmonary tuberculosis and spent the best part of the next 12 years in sanatoria and convalescence homes. When he finally recovered, he was already in his thirties. He had a degree in French and Classics and a few articles to his name, but little work experience and limited career prospects.

However, he had read extensively and a fellow patient had introduced him to Marxism. In Barthes's view, Marxism was the only theory that could produce an effective analysis of social institutions. Like countless people at the time, Barthes was an admirer of Jean-Paul Sartre, the left-wing philosopher and writer. Unlike Sartre, however, he never made the move from a critique of society to political activism. His was a flexible brand of Marxism and later he would feel at odds with what he regarded as the excesses of the violent, left-wing student rebellion of May 1968 in France.

From 1946 to 1960, Barthes took up a variety of short-term appointments. He worked as a librarian in Romania and a language assistant in Egypt. In France he was employed as a civil servant and then as a research assistant. It was during his stay at the University of Alexandria that Barthes was first introduced to linguistics by A.J. Greimas. He realized that the tools developed to analyse language would prove useful in his own work and consequently he always kept abreast of research in this field.

During this period Barthes published *Writing Degree Zero* (1953) and *Michelet* (1954), two books that reflect his early concerns with literature and history. He also wrote numerous articles for learned journals and newspapers. In fact, the pieces collected in *Mythologies* (1957), the book that made him famous, first appeared as articles in a magazine. The critique of bourgeois society and consumerism which Barthes proposed in *Mythologies* became influential and inspired journalists, filmmakers and novelists alike. He understood advertising so well that, unexpectedly, publicity houses took an interest in his book and used his methods to assess the quality of their own work.

The next time Barthes caused a stir in the media for altogether different reasons. In 1963 he published a collection of essays which offered new perspectives, some inspired by psychoanalysis, on the work of the seventeenth-century French dramatist Racine. Traditional scholars, who obviously felt that Classical French literature was their preserve, were incensed by the book. As long as Barthes concerned himself with 'trivia', the theatre of Bertold Brecht, or the experimental work of the new generation of French novelists who were making the headlines at the time, he could be ignored. Racine, however, was another matter. In 1965 Raymond Picard, a respected academic, published a pamphlet entitled *New Criticism or New Fraud?* which gave rise to a massive controversy in the press. Barthes's answer, *Criticism and Truth* (1966), was wide ranging and put forward a radically new agenda for literary studies.

By then Barthes was no longer an isolated figure. He had become associated with a variety of new journals. These attracted young researchers who would later play a leading role in the intellectual life of the country and disseminate Barthes's ideas. Barthes was also very close to the editor of *Tel Quel*, a review noted for its aggressive revolutionary stance and avant-garde activities. Thus Barthes became the symbol of all that was new and subversive at the time. He excelled at capturing the mood of the moment and his ideas became part of the spirit of the times. This was an era when essays in the human sciences could generate as much interest as works of literature and sell in comparable numbers.

From 1960 onwards, Barthes was fully immersed in academic life. He had been appointed in Paris at the École Pratique des Hautes Études, a somewhat marginal institution in the French university system, where he held weekly seminars. As years went by these seminars, which were initially attended by friends and admirers, attracted more and more students disaffected with the traditional academic system. The seminars were conducted in an atmosphere of intellectual freedom and exchange, most unusual in academic institutions at the time. From 1962 to 1976, Barthes used the seminars to experiment with ideas. They were the testing ground for his books and articles.

The late 1960s and early 1970s was the period when Barthes thought of himself first and foremost as a structuralist. He was intent on introducing scientific methods into the humanities. First, he established the foundations of semiology, the science of signs, in 'Elements of semiology' and *The Fashion System* (1967). Then he went on to produce seminal essays and books, most notably 'Introduction to the Structural Analysis of Narrative' and *S/Z* (1970), which provided the basis for the systematic analysis of literature. For many, to this day, the name of Barthes is synonymous with structuralism.

Up until this point, Barthes had been mainly concerned with meaning, uncovering myth, and revealing the systems that underpin and organize verbal or visual messages. But what about the subject, reader or viewer, without whom there is no meaning? Barthes surprised his followers by concentrating increasingly on issues of subjectivity and pleasure, most notably with the publication of *The Pleasure of the Text* (1973). Gradually he started writing without reference to theories like Marxism, psychoanalysis or semiology. Nevertheless Barthes's 'intuitions' remained as thought-provoking as ever. His *Roland Barthes* (1975) brought new life to the autobiographical genre and *A Lover's Discourse* (1977), which concentrated on the language of love at a time when 'sex' was the order of the day, reached a wide readership. Finally *Camera Lucida* (1980), which he wrote after the painful loss of his mother, contributed significantly to the debate on the nature of photography.

When he died in 1980, following a banal road accident, Barthes was at the height of his fame. National recognition had finally come to him in 1976 in the form of an election to the Collège de France, one of the most prestigious academic institutions in the country, where he held the chair of 'literary semiology'. The text of his inaugural lecture appeared in the national press and his lectures were hugely popular.

Barthes's appeal did not wane. Why? Because of his unique position in the recent history of ideas. Having spent many years away from centres of learning and the French literary scene, Barthes had a culture of his own and was not influenced by intellectual fashions. As he grew in confidence, he proposed new concepts, created trends and the critic became a hero. Regarded as a remarkable writer, Barthes was quoted, he was followed, and many of his ideas have now become accepted wisdom. At a time when the human sciences were elaborating increasingly sophisticated models and experimental literature was flourishing, Barthes mastered these theories and texts and made them available to broader audiences.

However, the influence he gained over the years never prevented Barthes from moving forward and finding new objectives and methods. The hallmark of his work is its diversity. Barthes seemed equally at ease when he revealed the meanings of everyday 'trivia', when he introduced the theatre of Brecht and Racine or the novels of experimental young French writers, when he discussed the work of a nineteenth-century historian such as Michelet or novelist such as Balzac, or when he wrote about cinema, photography, music or love. The same diversity is evident in his methods: first seen as a demanding Marxist, he promoted the use of critical tools developed in the fields of ethnology, psychoanalysis and linguistics; then having contributed to the development of a scientific approach to the humanities, he rehabilitated the value of pleasure in the appreciation of art and culture. As a result, Barthes's works remain a central point of reference in a diverse range of cultural debates. The following chapters will outline the evolution of Barthes's thinking with particular emphasis on those areas where he remains most influential today.

* * *SUMMARY* * *

- Roland Barthes (1915–1980) published his first book, *Writing Degree Zero*, in his late thirties and obtained his first permanent teaching post at the age of 45.

- He rose to fame with *Mythologies* (1957), a wide-ranging study of cultural phenomena, and his next book, *On Racine* (1963), created a massive controversy.

- Henceforth Barthes concentrated on introducing scientific methods into the humanities. 'Elements of Semiology' (1965) and *The Fashion System* (1967) established the foundations of 'semiology', the science of signs; and 'Introduction to the Structural Analysis of Narrative' (1966) and *S/Z* (1970) promoted the systematic analysis of literature. As a result, Barthes's name became synonymous with structuralism.

- From the early 1970s onwards however, Barthes gradually distanced himself from his previous endeavours and brought to the fore notions of pleasure and subjectivity, notably in *the Pleasure of the Text* (1973).

- With *Roland Barthes* (1975), his thought-provoking autobiographical essay, *A Lover's Discourse* (1977) and *Camera Lucida* (1980), he finally established himself as a creative writer.

- When he died in 1980, Barthes was at the height of his fame and, ever since, his work has provided key references in the humanities at large.

Mythologies 2

In 1952, Barthes started writing occasional feature articles on current cultural phenomena for the French press and from 1954 to 1956 he contributed a regular column on the same subject entitled 'Mythology of the Month' in *Les Lettres nouvelles*, a literary magazine. These brief journalistic pieces were eventually published as a collection of essays, *Mythologies* (1957), which made a strong impression at the time and remains, to this day, Barthes's most widely read work.

Mythologies is, in many ways, a chronicle of post-Second World War France. Barthes's ability to capture the spirit of the times – the 'zeitgeist' – certainly contributed to the initial popularity of the book. Its enduring success, however, is due to the breadth and variety of cultural phenomena that Barthes examined and his unique way of deciphering this material. In the 53 feature articles included in the book, we see Barthes repeatedly peeling off one layer of meaning after another, until he reaches what he deems to be the core significance of what he is analysing. The range of subjects covered in this process is most extraordinary: the world of wrestling; photographs of film actors; the way the Romans are pictured in film epics; writers on holiday; a royal cruise; literary critics; advertisements for cleaning powders; Charlie Chaplin's *Modern Times*; celebrities's weddings; the trial of an old man accused of murder; floods in Paris; French national foods; political speeches; jet plane pilots; cycling races; guidebooks for tourists; agony aunts; the new Citroën car; singing styles; astrology; and the photograph of a black soldier saluting the French flag, among many other topics.

Barthes's overall approach was highly influential. In the intellectual climate of France in the 1960s, demystifying the cultural messages that permeate society was considered a revolutionary project. In the

English-speaking world, from the 1970s onwards, his work was also discussed at length within the growing field of cultural studies.

CRITICAL DISTANCE

Mythologies was not Barthes's first book. *Michelet*, a literary analysis of the work of a prolific and influential nineteenth-century French historian, had appeared in 1954. And a year earlier, Barthes had published *Writing Degree Zero*, a collection of essays outlining a kind of 'History of French Writing' from the seventeenth century onwards.

Barthes's move from historical and literary studies to the analysis, in journalistic form, of what many would consider to be largely trivial, may seem surprising. The leap, nevertheless, is not as great as it might first appear. Whatever he examined, Barthes demonstrated the same ability and readiness to break down barriers and question prevalent assumptions. He considered both the products of 'high brow' culture and mass culture with an intensity of focus that showed them to be equally revealing and significant – a stance that was far from fashionable at the time. Furthermore, in order to make explicit hidden meanings and vested interests, Barthes used the kind of critical distance afforded by historical perspective.

Barthes's famous saying that 'where History is denied it is most clearly at work' reveals his preoccupation with the idea of history. Not because history repeats itself and lessons learnt from the past can be applied to the present, but because, over time, people's understanding of their position in society and the world at large changes. The resulting gulf between the past and the present needs, therefore, to be investigated and elucidated. For Barthes, the very distance that separates our values and assumptions from those of our forebears is the key to our understanding of both our past and our present. If what seemed absolutely natural to previous generations is so much at odds with what is taken for granted by current generations, it means that the values, assumptions and practices prevalent in any society at a particular point in time are a product of history. 'Ideology' is the term used to describe these values, assumptions and practices.

IDEOLOGY

The word **ideology** usually refers to a comprehensive and coherent set of basic ideas and beliefs about political, economic, social and cultural affairs, which members of a society hold in common. It is a shared and accepted 'vision of the world' which serves to describe, interpret and justify the place of a particular group or society in the grander scheme of things. In different societies or within the same society, there are various kinds of ideology: liberal, revolutionary, totalitarian, pacifist, racist, or feminist, for example.

KEYWORD

Ideology: generally ideas and beliefs about political, economic, social and cultural affairs, which members of a society hold in common. From a Marxist point of view, ideology is the cultural manifestation of the class system.

From the Marxist point of view adopted by Barthes in *Mythologies*, ideology is the product of social and economic interests. It is the cultural manifestation of the class system. Since dominant ideas within a society tend to be those of the dominant classes, ideology is one of the means used by these classes to oppress other social groups. An important characteristic of ideology is that it appears to be self-evident and it appeals to 'common sense'. As a result, it can lead people to believe that their position in society is part of the natural order of things. Indeed, as Barthes points out, the greater its apparent self-evidence, the greater its political potency as a tool of oppression.

LITERARY FORM AND IDEOLOGY

Barthes's interest in how ideology works initially appeared in *Writing Degree Zero*, where he outlines the emergence of a classical mode of writing in seventeenth-century France and its subsequent fate. This type of writing was praised for its unique precision, clarity and intelligibility, and came to be seen as the 'natural' way to represent reality. By the nineteenth century, it stood as the universal model for writing in France.

From the 1850s onwards, however, its influence started to wane, giving way to a range of new forms. Why? Barthes suggests that its decline coincided with the economic, social and political upheavals that shook the French bourgeois-led society during the 1840s. This coincidence implies that classical French writing was the result of specific historical circumstances and hence not as self-evident, natural and inevitable as it was originally claimed to be. It was not reflecting reality in the only possible way, it was emphatically moulding reality in the interests of the dominant classes – lawyers, merchants and politicians generally. It was a reflection of both their aspirations and self-confidence, with which writers readily identified.

The rise of modern capitalism and the beginnings of socialism undermined such identification and, as writers felt the need to redefine their position in relation to dominant ideology, new forms of writing appeared and proliferated. Their political significance was not simply derived from their content or their authors' stated political allegiances, but from their formal characteristics. Even the supposedly neutral style of writing adopted by contemporaries of Barthes, the 'degree zero' of writing that gives its title to his book, can never be totally neutral or non-committal. In the final analysis, no writing can be altogether devoid of an ideological dimension and this is why Barthes sees writing as 'an act of historical solidarity'.

MYTH

Having stressed the ideological implications of literary discourse, Barthes went on to show in *Mythologies* that the same is true of all kinds of messages circulating in society. By 'message', he meant not only verbal messages but anything that has meaning. This included, among many other things: images (films, photographs, advertisements); attitudes or patterns of behaviour (views on crime, racial prejudice, approaches to food, love and sentimentality); specific actions or events (a striptease act, a cycling race, an industrial strike, an exhibition); as well as everyday objects (a new car, toys, an item of clothing, a tobacco pipe).

One of the many **myths** exposed by Barthes concerned a curate nicknamed 'Abbé Pierre' who fought for the socially excluded and homeless in the 1950s and in the process became what we would now call a 'media icon'. Commenting on Abbé Pierre's physical appearance, Barthes singled out his

KEYWORD

Myth: a message or cultural representation which appears to be 'natural' but is, in fact, motivated by ideology.

nondescript haircut – short but not styled – and long beard. His haircut, as well as his overall demeanour, probably stemmed from a genuine disregard for appearance and fashion. But once Abbé Pierre achieved public notoriety through the media, his unassuming haircut stopped being just a haircut. It took on a new, second-order meaning: no longer the 'neutral' appearance of a humble curate, it became the very image of neutrality, the unmistakable sign of Abbé Pierre's humility and sanctity.

The same could be said of Abbé Pierre's long, untrimmed beard, but for different reasons. It was unusual for parish priests to wear beards and, in religious imagery, beards tend to refer back to an older and purer form of religious belief, conjuring up images of missionary zeal and self-imposed poverty. Through this type of conventional association, Abbé Pierre's beard became the sign that he was a new Francis of Assisi and compounded the effect of the haircut. As a result, a myth – in the Barthesian sense – was born.

What was the purpose of this myth? Barthes's interpretation of it is that while the public took in, i.e. 'consumed', the signs of charity and admired the saintly zeal of Abbé Pierre, they did not question the uses and limitations of charity. They saw it as the natural solution to the endemic, inevitable, problem of poverty and homelessness. By losing sight of the real causes of social deprivation at that particular point in time, they did not look for political solutions. Hence the signs of charity had become a moral alibi and a substitute for social justice.

Here, as in all the other pieces included in *Mythologies*, Barthes is at pains to show that anyone and anything can take on mythical meanings, reflecting dominant ideology. Barthes is not interested in Abbé Pierre, the man of flesh and bone, but in his image. However 'innocent' and good his intentions – which would give his actions their first-order meaning – the second-order meanings attached to his image, serve the purpose of what Barthes calls 'petit-bourgeois' ideology. They support the status quo as a natural, indeed inevitable, state of affairs, which is beyond question.

THE ENDURING PRESENCE OF MYTHS

The examples of myths cited by Barthes cannot always be transposed easily or succinctly to the present day or to the English-speaking world. Let us imagine, however, what Barthes might have to say about more recent media personalities and cultural phenomena.

Barthes was interested in the way individuals whose social status and/or achievements set them apart from humanity at large, are presented as superhuman, god-like figures. He demonstrated, for instance, that far from bringing them down to the level of mere mortals, showing celebrities engaged in mundane, neutral activities such as eating, shaving and relaxing tends to highlight that they are indeed very special. When they appear to behave like normal people, they seem even more miraculous – they can only be superhuman because they are first of all human. A recent photograph showing an acclaimed international footballer apparently hosing down an immaculate, shiny, silver-coloured racing car – a mythical object in itself – was a clear reminder of Barthes's point. Seeing the footballer seemingly engaged in an act of mundane drudgery made his achievements even more extraordinary, thus justifying the level of his earnings to his considerably poorer supporters.

Another example of prevalent myth is the way women are represented in the media. In 'Novels and Children' Barthes points out that, in a recent survey of female novelists published by a woman's magazine, the writers are identified not only by the number of books they have produced but also by the number of children they have: 'Jacqueline Lenoir (two daughters, one novel); Marina Grey (one son, one novel), Nicole Dutreil (two sons, four novels)…'. Barthes reads this as an encouragement for women to be free, creative and productive in the market-place while, at the same time, reminding them that this freedom is a luxury and that their prime role is to produce children (which, in the sentence quoted by Barthes, come before books); men are not mentioned explicitly but nevertheless define the condition of these women. Half a century later, we may have the impression that this view of women and their role in society has radically changed. However, the example of wives of presidents and prime ministers in Western democracies seems to show that the myth of womanhood is evolving but has not disappeared. Today, First Ladies – and the word 'ladies' as opposed to 'women' or 'wives' is clearly reminiscent of antiquated attitudes – are increasingly visible. Whatever their own professional achievements, though, they tend to only appear on formal occasions, in domestic settings, and in caring or supportive roles. There are indeed examples of female presidents and prime ministers, but it is significant that the phrase 'First Gentleman' is never used to refer to the husband of a head of state; husbands rarely appear officially in the supportive role unless their own achievements can be used as a form of endorsement. Even today, First Ladies often comply with the mythical view of women as standing, metaphorically and literally, *by* their 'man'.

These analyses of more recent phenomena corroborate the Barthesian view that myths may evolve but remain, nevertheless, all-pervasive.

DEMYSTIFICATION

For Barthes, the function of the mythologists, as opposed to that of the myth-makers, was to counter myths by exposing them as delusions or lies. Although not a revolutionary in the strictly Marxist sense – he did not advocate the violent overthrow of the government of the day – Barthes was sympathetic to the Marxist cause and considered myth as essentially conservative. He wished to open the eyes of the public to the fact that what might appear 'innocent' and 'perfectly natural' was largely the result of distortion and misrepresentation. He thought that demystification would successfully weaken the power of myth and the powerful economic and political interests that it served.

In spite of the success of *Mythologies*, Barthes failed in his political purpose. Far from being discredited as a misrepresentation, if not a lie, 'image' as a mythical construct is now a recognized and fully accepted aspect of social life. For instance, awareness that myths are used to promote sales of particular products does not necessarily make these items any less desirable. We even judge the worth and professionalism of our public figures on their ability as myth-makers. Any failure in this respect is seen as an intrinsic lack of sophistication and resourcefulness.

Barthes succeeded, nonetheless, in challenging the conventional view of culture as confined to the library, the concert hall and the theatre, and he extended it in a way that encompassed all aspects of everyday life. This was truly a ground-breaking achievement.

* * *SUMMARY* * *

● What seemed absolutely natural to previous generations is often very different from what is taken for granted today. This is because the values, assumptions and practices prevalent in any society at a particular point in time are a product of history.

● The term used to describe these values, assumptions and practices is 'ideology'.

● Since dominant ideas are usually those of the dominant social group, ideology is, from Barthes's Marxist point of view, one of the means used by the dominant classes to oppress other groups.

● Myths are all those messages or cultural representations that appear harmlessly 'natural' and are, in fact, motivated by ideology.

● No cultural phenomenon is altogether free of ideological implications and anything can take on mythical meanings.

● For Barthes, the function of the mythologist is to counter myths by exposing them as lies.

3 Semiology

Mythologies ends with a theoretical essay entitled 'Myth Today', which provides, retrospectively, unity and direction to the collection of articles. The main function of this concluding essay is to express, in more general terms, the links between the various descriptive pieces written by Barthes in the preceding years. It adds little to our understanding of the individual pieces which stand perfectly well on their own. The essay's true significance comes from the fact that, in order to explain how myth works, Barthes turned to linguistics and thus discovered semiology.

In 'Myth Today', Barthes explains that his main concern is not with the content of myths, i.e. particular meanings or types of meanings. Neither does he wish to differentiate between the means that convey those mythical meanings – language, images, objects, behaviour. His main purpose, at this stage, is to examine how mythical meaning itself is conveyed.

MYTH AS A SYSTEM OF COMMUNICATION

In the various analyses leading up to 'Myth Today', myth essentially appears as a kind of distorted representation. In this concluding essay, Barthes approaches the issue from a much more general angle, that of communication. He stresses that myth is 'neither an object, a concept, nor an idea', but an 'act of speech' ('an utterance'). This means that myth, in the Barthesian sense, is not defined by its content – its meanings – but by the particular way in which it delivers that content. Barthes suggests that, as a form capable of conveying meaning, myth is a specific system of communication.

Language was the only type of communication that had been studied systematically until then and so Barthes turned to linguistics in his search for appropriate analytical tools to tackle myth.

He found these in the work of Ferdinand de Saussure, the founding figure of modern linguistics. Saussure was a Swiss linguist whose findings became widely available after his death, thanks to the publication of his *Course in General Linguistics* (1915), compiled by his students from their lecture notes. Saussure's theory of language was immensely influential and provided the impetus for most of the research in linguistics in the twentieth century. The implications of Saussure's work are so wide ranging that they will be presented here in two stages. This chapter will concentrate on his definition of the linguistic sign, as adopted by Barthes in 'Myth Today'; and Chapter 5 will examine the broader implications of Saussure's view of language as a system of signs, not only for Barthes but for the humanities as a whole from the 1950s onwards.

SAUSSURE'S DEFINITION OF THE LINGUISTIC SIGN

Saussure describes the linguistic sign as a 'double entity, one formed by the association of two terms'. These two terms do not consist of a name and a thing, but of a form which signifies – the **signifier** – and a meaning – the **signified**. The two are as inseparable as the two sides of a single sheet of paper. The signifier is the

> **KEYWORDS**
>
> Sign: the association of a form (the signifier) and a meaning (the signified).

perceptible, material, acoustic or visual signal which triggers a mental image, i.e. the signified. Hence the signified of *cat* is not the animal itself, but a mental representation of a feline creature – the image we construct mentally when we hear the word or see it written. The signifier and the signified are linked by an associative bond *in the mind* and thus the resulting linguistic **sign** is described as a 'two-sided psychological entity'.

As already mentioned, Saussure's definition of the sign was extremely influential, not only in the field of linguistic research but in literature and the humanities in general. His theories were discussed, extended and confronted with other theories – notably those of American philosopher Charles Sanders Peirce – and, in the process, refined to account for the complexities of language and other types of communication. Saussure's definition of the linguistic sign as a double-sided entity (signifier/signified) has remained, nevertheless, a constant point of reference.

THE MYTHICAL SIGN

Barthes extended Saussure's definition of the sign to account for myth using a variety of examples. Here, for the purpose of clarity, we shall apply the model proposed by Barthes to one of the myths analysed in Chapter 2.

In the case of Abbé Pierre's haircut, the signifier is the visual stimulus received by our brain when we look at the man himself or at a photograph of him. If our vision or our mental faculties are not impaired, this signifier is interpreted as 'hair cut in a particular way'. The signified 'hair cut in a particular way' is, in this case, the first step in the process of meaning, i.e. a first-order signified.

With myth, the visual stimulus interpreted as a haircut, i.e. the haircut as a sign, triggers in turn another meaning, the concept of humility. This signified is, as we saw in Chapter 2, a second-order meaning. This is why Barthes referred to myth as a second-order system of signs or 'second-order semiological system'.

DENOTATION AND CONNOTATION

Barthes later revised his terminology and talked about 'denotated meaning' (or **denotation**) for first-order meaning, and 'connotated meaning' (or **connotation**) for second-order meaning. Although you may find that notions of 'first-order' and 'second-order' are clearer reminders of how Barthes saw myth, it is important to understand the terms 'denotation' and

KEYWORDS

Denotation: first-order meaning, basic meaning.

Connotation: second-order meaning based on association of ideas.

'connotation' because, following Barthes's example, they are now widely used to analyse all kinds of messages. The two terminologies will serve here to explain some of the key characteristics of the two different types of meaning, as exemplified in myth.

The main difference between the two is that denotation, or first-order meaning, is stable – a haircut is always a haircut. Whereas connotation, or second-order meaning, depends on context. In a different situation, and/or at a different time, a haircut similar to that of Abbé Pierre's could be perceived, for example, as a daring hairstyle and therefore connote not 'humility' but 'arrogance'.

Another important consideration is that several signs may carry the same connotation. For instance, we have seen that Abbé Pierre's haircut and beard conveyed similar meanings. Connotation, or second-order meaning, is somehow more general, more diffuse, than denotation. In the case of Abbé Pierre, ideas of 'humility', 'missionary zeal' and 'sanctity' were evoked. This is because connotation is fundamentally ideological – 'cultural' in the broadest sense of the word – and results from an association of ideas. It stems from the vision of the world that we share with people from the same cultural, social and/or historical background and is consequently based on convention. This conventional aspect of myth, made Saussure's findings all the more relevant to Barthes's project.

THE ARBITRARY NATURE OF THE SIGN

In his definition of the linguistic sign, Saussure stressed its **arbitrary** nature. By insisting that the sign is arbitrary, he meant that there is no natural connection between the signifier and the signified. There is no intrinsic or essential reason why any particular combination of sounds or letters should be linked to any particular concept.

> **KEYWORD**
>
> Arbitrary: there is no natural connection between the signifier and the signified in language.

The associative bond between them is not based on natural resemblance; it is simply an accepted convention.

The arbitrary nature of the linguistic sign is evidenced by the fact that there is no single universal language in the world. Instead, there are different languages, which have developed different signs and different links between signifiers and signifieds. Even when similar words exist in two languages, they may have different meanings. For example, the signified of 'chair' is 'seat' for English speakers, whereas 'chair' means 'flesh' for French speakers. Furthermore, onomatopoeia and interjections – words whose sounds supposedly imitate what they refer to – are also, at least partly, conventional. For instance, the rooster's call is 'cock-a-doodle-do' for the English, 'cocorico' for the French and 'quiquiriqui' for the Spanish; where an English speaker says 'ouch!', a French speaker says 'aïe!'.

When we learn a language, we inherit ready-made links between signifier and signified, which we then take for granted and may even consider as 'natural'. Similarly, we inherit or acquire the values and assumptions of the social group or society to which we belong, and henceforth behave as if they were self-evident. Just as Saussure stressed that the link between signifier and signified is not based on natural resemblance but on convention, Barthes was at pains to show that everyday life is riddled with myths based on cultural conventions and that the function of these myths is to make us mistake culture for nature.

SEMIOLOGY

Having discovered that linguistic terms and concepts were offering new perspectives on cultural phenomena, Barthes came to the idea that all human activity could perhaps be studied as a series of languages, i.e. as systems of signs. Thus his study of myths led Barthes to consider the notion of a general science of signs postulated by Saussure: **semiology**.

Saussure thought of language as part of a larger communication framework. He therefore saw the study of language – linguistics – as part of a much broader science that would study 'the life of all signs within society'. He called this new discipline, which would include linguistics, semiology. Saussure did not go any further in establishing this new area of research, however. Instead, he concentrated on linguistics. His reasoning was that language has a privileged position as the most complex and universal of all semiological systems, as well as the most characteristic. He believed that semiology would inevitably be dependent upon the study of language, which would provide the key, the 'master-pattern', for all branches of semiology.

Although Saussure had many disciples across Europe from the 1920s onwards, this aspect of his work was ignored for nearly half a century. One of Barthes's major contributions to late twentieth-century thought is that he realized the potential of Saussure's idea and set about developing semiology into a fully fledged science. In order to define the new discipline, he tested analytical concepts drawn from linguistics on other cultural phenomena: image-based signifying practices such as photography or cinema, and object-based practices such as clothes or food. In each instance, he would specify the signifier and the signified and attempt to define the relationship between the two. He would also spell out the denotation of the messages under scrutiny and make their connotations explicit. However dry a task this may appear to us now, it was a most exciting undertaking, which aroused great enthusiasm as well as controversy. Never before had there been such a systematic attempt to make explicit what we know implicitly and hence reassess familiar everyday practices.

Barthes's findings were first published in *Elements of Semiology* (1965) which served as a blueprint for the future development of semiology. It was a short, theoretical book in which Barthes put forward the basic analytical concepts drawn from linguistics, which were general enough to account for all systems of signs: the distinction between signifier and signified; the difference between denotation and connotation; the relevance of the notion of arbitrariness. Barthes also stressed the importance of the interaction between the elements within each system and between these elements and the system itself, as explained in Chapter 5.

Then, in 1967, came *The Fashion System*, a hefty tome written between 1957 and 1963, which combined theory with practice. It was the closest Barthes ever came to academic writing and fortunately for his readers, as some critics said, he never repeated the exercise. It is not so much the complexity of the book that made for a tedious read, but Barthes's uncharacteristic style of writing, the extent of his detailed analyses and his general approach to female fashion. Barthes had no interest in fashion as an enhancer of the female body, nor in the clothes themselves. His main interest was in the way clothing is made socially meaningful. He had originally intended to study the clothes themselves or pictures of them, but he soon realized that things only exist in our minds once they have been named and that their meaning has to be put into words to be grasped. He therefore came to the conclusion that it is the way clothes are described in fashion magazines that makes them appear distinctive and especially desirable to particular groups of women. As a result, his study of fashion was based entirely on the close analysis of captions describing photographs of clothes in fashion magazines.

This confirmed to Barthes the idea that, contrary to Saussure's belief, linguistics was not a branch of semiology but, on the contrary, a general science which included semiology. This belief that our experience of the world is always mediated by language would have a decisive influence on the future course of Barthes's work and the future of semiology as a whole.

LANGUAGE AND THOUGHT

Throughout the twentieth century, the question of the relationship between language and thought has been the subject of much debate. For some, language is essentially determined by society, culture and people's general view of 'reality'. For others, instead of reflecting reality, language organizes 'reality'. Barthes was not directly involved in this debate, but like many of his contemporaries, he tended to favour the latter proposition.

Like Saussure, he did not view words and thoughts as separate, but as inextricably bound together. This is because language is not simply a nomenclature, i.e. a list of names matching a list of pre-existing concepts. If that was the case, all languages would provide word for word equivalents for each concept. But as we know, it is not quite that simple. For example, different languages approach colour in different ways: from one language to another, the names of colours never quite correspond. What is perceived as one colour in one language, may be perceived differently in another. For English speakers, the internal part of an egg is yellow – 'yolk' is derived from the Old English word for yellow – the same is true for the French who call it 'le jaune'. However, the Italians call it 'il rosso' and therefore perceive it as red. In this instance, sensitivity to colour is, at least partly, programmed by language.

This means that when we learn a language, we acquire a certain view of the world – a particular way of thinking about reality. If, in order to think, we need words and if these words already carry a particular conception of the world, then language is bound to shape the way we think.

THE FUTURE OF SEMIOLOGY

Although fascinated by language, Barthes was not a linguist and never claimed to be. Just as he turned to Saussure for a definition of the sign, he studied the work of many linguists, borrowing, for example, the concepts of denotation and connotation from the Danish linguist Louis Hjelmslev (1899–1965). In the process of establishing semiology, Barthes alienated the sympathies of many established linguists but fired the enthusiasm of a whole generation who set about analyzing systematically the entire range of 'signifying practices' that make up culture, from food to town planning, from literature to medicine and from cinema to comics.

Barthes himself did not produce any other large-scale semiological analysis after *The Fashion System*, and he eventually came to question its premise (see Chapter 6). Having laid down the theoretical foundations of semiology, which flourished under the name of **semiotics** and came to occupy a dominant position in the humanities, Barthes chose not to reap the benefits that the enhanced status of the new science would have given him. Instead, he retired to its margins.

From the late 1960s onwards, Barthes focused his attention increasingly on language and literature and, while retaining the term 'semiology' to describe his activities, came to redefine its function. The object of semiology was no longer the scientific analysis of meaning, but the study of phenomena that resist scientific analysis. True to himself, once semiology had become an established discipline, and so part of dominant ideology, Barthes questioned its authority.

KEYWORDS

Two words are used to refer to the 'study of signs':

Semiology: coined by the Swiss linguist Ferdinand de Saussure (1857–1913).

Semiotics: derived from research into symbols carried out independently by American philosopher Charles Sanders Peirce (1839–1914).

Although Saussure's theories had a greater impact on the original development of the new discipline than Peirce's, semiotics has now become the preferred term.

Barthes's subsequent attitude to what he had set in motion, did not diminish its impact in any way. While *Mythologies* extended the notion of culture to all aspects of everyday life, Barthes's semiology gave his contemporaries and successive generations the desire and the tools needed to investigate how cultural practices, whatever form they may take, create meaning. His achievement in this respect was enormous and his legacy endures.

❋ ❋ ❋ *SUMMARY* ❋ ❋ ❋

● Barthes came to the conclusion that myth is not defined by its content – its meanings – but the way it delivers its content.

● He therefore defined myth as a particular system of communication – a kind of language – and used Ferdinand de Saussure's *Course in General Linguistics* (1915) as the starting point for his analysis of how myth works.

● Saussure had expressed, but not developed, the view that the study of language is part of the broad study of all signs in society – semiology.

● Barthes took up this idea and laid down the foundations of semiology – a new discipline whose function is to describe the system of rules and distinctions that make meaning possible.

4 New criticism

Throughout his career, Barthes never ceased to be a literary critic. *Mythologies*, which went far beyond the then accepted notions of culture, included several analyses of prevalent attitudes to literature and, while pursuing his study of the fashion system, Barthes also produced a number of works focusing on literary issues.

For instance, one of the literary essays included in *Mythologies* was devoted to Jean Racine, the seventeenth-century French dramatist. It was entitled 'Racine is Racine', a phrase which summed up, in Barthes's view, the way that works of the past were, generally and mistakenly, presented. For Barthes, 'Racine is Racine', is the French equivalent of 'Shakespeare is Shakespeare', the kind of tautological statement that is commonly used to cut short any discussion and suppress all possible debate. It implies that there is only one way of understanding Racine. It takes Racine's work for granted, wrongly suggesting that it is transparent and self-evident – a universally understood entity – and that there is an unquestionable 'truth' about Racine. The purpose of such a statement, from Barthes's point of view, was to stifle curiosity, justify thoughtlessness, and generally promote intellectual apathy. It was as though thinking itself was threatening and must be resisted at all cost. That was enough for Barthes to suggest that one should actively think about Racine.

NEW INTERPRETATIONS OF PAST MASTERPIECES
In the years following *Mythologies*, Barthes published three essays on Racine's tragedies, which appeared together in 1963 under the title *On Racine*. In his foreword to the book, Barthes explains that his concern is not with Racine himself but with Racine's heroes, asserting that his analyses avoid using biographical and historical evidence or, as he puts it, 'inferring from the work to the author and from the author to the

work'. He discusses Racine's tragedies *from the inside*, without any reference to the biography of the dramatist and the times in which he lived. He uses psychoanalysis and formal analysis to understand the characters and the manner in which they interact. Barthes claims, for example, that it is pointless to discuss whether one of the female characters is a coquette or her male counterpart the epitome of virility. He would rather express their relationship in abstract terms, such as 'A has power over B, A loves B who does not return her/his affection', and discuss love in terms of sexual desire.

We have grown accustomed to modern interpretations of works of the past. However, at the time, Barthes's exploration of the meaning of seventeenth-century plays from a twentieth-century theoretical or philosophical standpoint was part of a much more recent and radical trend. When the book came out, some reviewers saw it as an exciting and refreshing point of view: they congratulated Barthes on the way he reassessed the meaning of Racinian tragedy and shed light on previously undiscovered aspects of Racine's work. Meanwhile, other critics responded negatively and sarcastically wondered how Barthes had managed to unearth meanings of which no one, not even Racine himself, had been aware. Although, retrospectively, it can be said that Barthes's essays on Racine were not as ground breaking and influential as some of the structural analyses he would later promote, *On Racine* marked a turning point in his thinking, and created quite a stir at the time.

The controversy flared up again in 1964 with the publication of *Critical Essays*. As a result of this collection of essays, Barthes emerged as the spokesman of a new, modern, kind of literary criticism. He touched on subjects ranging from Greek classical theatre to the experimental work of young French writers, which soon came to be known as *le nouveau roman* (the New Novel). Barthes also discussed the writings of French authors of the three previous centuries, as well as those of the twentieth-century German dramatist Bertold Brecht and Czech writer Franz Kafka. However, what particularly incensed Barthes's detractors were two essays about French literary criticism, originally published in

English. In the first of these articles, Barthes established a distinction between what he called French **academic criticism** and new forms of interpretative criticism; while in the second one, he tried to define more precisely the aims and functions of this new kind of interpretation.

KEYWORD

Academic criticism: literary analysis based on nineteenth-century notions of cause and effect, which looks for the meaning of the work in the biography of the author.

CONVENTIONAL LITERARY CRITICISM

What Barthes called 'academic criticism' was an approach steeped in nineteenth-century philosophical traditions. This approach stemmed from the assumption that all knowledge must be based on fact and observation (positivism) and that all human actions and choices are determined by preceding events or situations (determinism). Although philosophy had moved on since then, the French university system had not. The way academics were recruited and promoted was not conducive to exploration and innovation, and in the early 1960s the view of literature perpetuated by the French academic system was still based on these outdated nineteenth-century models. Literature was seen as the product of particular individuals living at specific moments in history, who had something to 'express'. Writers would take pen to paper because they had something to say and the function of writing was to express their sensibilities and passions. Therefore, the role of criticism was to uncover the original intention of the author in order to find the 'true' meaning of the text. To achieve this, academic critics undertook long and painstaking studies of an author's biography, sources and socio-political background, which were seen as keys to the understanding of literary works. They relied, for this purpose, on historical scholarship and a fairly simplistic form of psychology.

Barthes's fundamental objection to this critical approach was that, although it stressed the importance of history as a determining factor in literature, it ignored the lessons of history which tells us that nothing is beyond time nor everlastingly universal. This was not a new development in Barthes's thought: such arguments appear time and time again in *Writing degree Zero* and *Mythologies*. For Barthes, any kind of claim to universal truth was a sure sign of ideological motivation. In this case, he saw academic criticism as serving the interests of the university system by preserving its privileged position as the custodian of a body of knowledge. The 'academic' approach tended to mummify the work, turn it into some kind of historical monument, which provided a convenient basis for the testing of students and the conferring of qualifications. Barthes's own view was that literature and art generally belong to both the past and the present, and that the full meaning of particular works is not necessarily realized at the time when they appear. Because texts outlive their authors, they carry on being read and interpreted by readers at different times, and their meaning is constantly evolving. Ultimately, it is not the intention of the author that makes a book valuable, but its ability to create new readings and new debate at any given moment.

Barthes also pointed out that, instead of focusing on particular works, academic criticism always studied them in relation to something else, outside the work: the author's literary influences or sources; personal experiences or feelings; and social or political background. The emphasis was always on similarities between the author's life and times (seen as causes) and his works (seen as effects). A character would be viewed as representing the author or someone the author loved or hated, fictional events would be said to mirror some of the author's experiences, and fiction was generally regarded as imitating reality. When the critic failed to identify appropriate parallels and this simplistic model thus failed to provide insights into the work, the critic would then often invoke the 'genius' of the author to account for any form of unpredictability. Although Freud had uncovered some of the complexities of the human psyche and shown the importance, for instance, of 'denial' as an emotional mechanism, academic critics tended to ignore the possibility that authors might show one of their characters as infatuated not because they were themselves in love, but in order to compensate for the fact that they were not. Even when academic critics could countenance such a possibility, they still used psychoanalysis to uncover hidden truths in isolated episodes, and to relate these to the biography of the author. In both instances, they were focusing on exterior causes to explain the work, instead of looking at the work as a whole and focusing on the internal workings of the text in order to make its inherent meanings explicit.

NEW FORMS OF LITERARY CRITICISM

While Barthes objected to the attempt by academic criticism to hide its ideological motivations, he praised the more recent forms of criticism for acknowledging that all approaches inevitably reflect particular assumptions. *La nouvelle critique* (New Criticism) came in different forms but always spoke from a distinctive and explicit point of view. Having chosen to use one of the modern approaches available to them – existentialism, Marxism, psycho-analysis – the new critics tested the validity of their approach by describing established works anew to see what new meanings might emerge.

KEYWORD

La nouvelle critique: literary criticism based explicitly on twentieth-century approaches such as Marxism, psycho-analysis or existentialism.

N.B. Although there are some similarities, *la nouvelle critique* that appeared in France in the 1960s is not to be confused with the New Criticism that emerged in the US and Britain in the 1930s and 1940s.

Barthes cited, among others, Gaston Bachelard (1884–1962) and Lucien Goldmann (1913–1970), as examples of critics to be emulated, among others. Bachelard did not focus on the work of particular writers but enquired into the literary mind in general, relating poetic symbols to the four natural elements – fire, water, earth and air – and studying them from a psychoanalytical perspective. Goldmann, on the other hand, was a Marxist critic who rejected the notion that literary works 'reflect' society. He posited instead that great works of literature reproduce unconsciously the way in which societies are organized and that there is a correlation, for instance, between the history of the novel form and the history of economic life in Western societies.

The aim of these critics was not to decipher works in order to find a hidden, secret meaning that no one had noticed until then, but to apply different grids of interpretation to see what particular meanings could be produced. The function of their various critical approaches was not to discover truths but to put forward valid interpretations of literature, i.e. readings that were coherent within their chosen framework. In this context, literature was not perceived as having one meaning but, depending on the approach used, several possible meanings. These meanings were not superimposed, but emerged and were made explicit through the scrutiny of the internal workings of the texts, what Barthes called **immanent** analysis. Only then did the critics turn their attention outwards to see how literature might make sense of the world.

> **KEYWORDS**
>
> **Immanent:** focusing exclusively on the internal workings of the text in order to make its inherent meanings explicit.

THE 'OLD GUARD' STRIKES BACK

Barthes's objections to academic criticism and his defence of new forms of literary interpretation did not go unnoticed. As a reaction to *On Racine* and *Critical Essays*, Raymond Picard, a lecturer in French literature at the university of Paris (La Sorbonne), saw fit to publish a 150-page critique entitled *New Criticism or New Fraud?* (1965). Picard was an eminent Racine scholar, one of the practitioners of the academic criticism that Barthes had called into question. Not only did he object to Barthes's readings, most notably his emphasis on sexuality in Racine and his use of jargon, he also viewed Barthes's *Critical Essays* as an attack against the French university system itself. Picard's virulent accusations found strong support in the national newspapers. Ironically, this expression of outrage confirmed Barthes's suggestion that, from an ideological point of view, there was much at stake behind traditional academic criticism and its claim to have a monopoly on truth.

Fundamentally, the debate was not about particular works of literature but about how much freedom the critic can or cannot exercise when interpreting literature. It was about freedom in relation to established values. Since the late 1950s, the political and social atmosphere had been particularly stifling in France. The authoritarianism of President de Gaulle was matched only by the authoritarianism of the main opposition party, the pro-Stalin Communist Party. Anti-authoritarian feeling was riding high and a new sense of individualism was emerging in a society that was undergoing rapid change. The battle between the old and the new values, that would eventually lead to the student revolt of May 1968, was gathering momentum. Barthes's writings were definitely on the side of the new: they were regarded as promoting change, undermining venerated institutions and attacking the establishment in general.

A SCIENTIFIC APPROACH TO LITERATURE

Barthes's response to Picard's diatribe was indirect but radical: a book entitled *Criticism and Truth* (1966). In this work, Barthes answered some of his opponents' criticisms, developed some of the ideas rehearsed in previous essays, and then put forward a clear-sighted programme for a structuralist science of literature, based on the linguistic model.

The mid-twentieth century had seen various attempts to bridge the traditional gap between the 'exact sciences' and the so-called 'human sciences'. In 1956, however, the scientific study of literature was still 'far more an aspiration than a reality', as Lucien Goldmann wrote. This was essentially due to the lack of agreement on the actual object of study and the methodology to be used. *Criticism and Truth* addressed these issues and the solutions proposed by Barthes cleared the way for fundamentally new developments which altered the course of literary studies.

Barthes argued that if we accept that a work of literature has a concrete material existence – that it is made up of writing – then a particular kind of science of literature – poetics – is possible. Like linguistics, it would proceed by deduction and put forward a hypothetical descriptive model outlining the rules that enable symbolic meanings to emerge. Its function would not be to impose any particular meaning on a work of literature, but to study the way in which writing produces meaning, regardless of what that meaning may be. This science of literature would not be concerned with authors and the contents of their works, but focus instead on forms. It would not seek to understand why and how works of literature came about but why they made, and continue to make, sense to their readers.

✳ ✳ ✳SUMMARY✳ ✳ ✳

● Barthes's *On Racine* (1963) analysed famous seventeenth-centuries plays from a twentieth-century perspective.

● His *Critical Essays* (1964) included articles attacking traditional literary criticism which relied on the study of the life and times of the author.

● Both books promoted new forms of literary criticism based on twentieth-century theoretical and philosophical approaches and, as such, provoked an angry reaction from traditionalists such as Raymond Picard.

● Barthes's answer to Picard's *New Criticism or New Fraud?* was a book entitled *Criticism and Truth* (1966).

● Most importantly, *Criticism and Truth* provided a programme for a structuralist science of literature that focused not on the meanings of particular works but on how meaning is made possible by literary forms.

5 Structuralism

Semiology and Barthes's programme for a science of literature are inextricably linked to the French structuralist movement in the social sciences and the humanities.

Although, strictly speaking, semiology was the science of signs, whereas **structuralism** was a method of analysis, the two terms were almost synonymous for a while in the 1960s. The confusion between semiology and structuralism stemmed from the fact that both originated in the work of Ferdinand de Saussure and his structural linguistics, and both had their heyday around 1966. Barthes was not unique in his approach. He shared it, at the time, with a number of other influential thinkers, who also placed themselves under the umbrella term of structuralism, adapting Saussure's theories to their own fields of enquiry. Most notably, anthropology (Claude Lévi-Strauss), psychoanalysis (Jacques Lacan), Marxist theory (Louis Althusser), history of ideas (Michel Foucault) and philosophy (Jacques Derrida). Because of their common ground, the cross-fertilization between the various disciplines was intense.

KEYWORDS

Structure: a system in which everything is related to everything else.

Structuralism: an approach that analyses and interprets its material (language, literature, society) as a system in order to discover universal organizing principles.

In Chapter 3, we saw how Barthes used Saussure's definition of the linguistic sign to account for myth and other cultural phenomena. In order to understand structuralism in general, and Barthes's approach in particular, we need to examine the general framework within which Saussure came to define the linguistic sign and the broader implications of his view of language as a system of signs.

LANGUAGE AS A STRUCTURE

There are so many different aspects of language that Saussure came to the conclusion that studying language in general was an impossible task. He therefore proceeded to define more precisely the object of what would become structural linguistics.

First, he introduced a distinction between **synchronic** analysis – a study of language at one point in time – and **diachronic** analysis – a study of language as it changes over time. Given that language always evolves piecemeal with a limited number of changes at any one time, the main characteristic of the diachronic approach is that it singles out those elements that change, and thus it does not view language as a whole. This is why Saussure opted for the synchronic approach, which enabled him to observe stable phenomena – the state of language at a particular time – and to concentrate on the overall picture.

KEYWORDS

Diachronic: over a period of time.

Synchronic: at one point in time.

Language: the linguistic code.

Speech: the linguistic code put to use, i.e. particular messages or utterances.

Second, Saussure introduced a fundamental distinction between **language** (*langue*) and **speech** (*parole*). 'Language' was the system itself – the code – whereas 'speech' was the system put to use – particular 'utterances' or 'messages', whether spoken or written. Here again, Saussure's own concern was with the general – language with its conventions, rules and norms – rather than with the particular – the individual acts of communication made possible by the language system. He pointed out that one of the fundamental characteristics of 'language', as opposed to 'speech', is that it is unconscious: when we speak we are aware of the content of the message we are communicating, but we are unaware of the underlying system that enables us to communicate this message – we use it unconsciously. In other words, it is not the content of the message that is unconscious, but the form. It was this emphasis on the unconscious nature of the system that made Saussure's findings relevant to approaches as diverse as Freudianism and Marxism; it provided bridges between different approaches and enabled cross-fertilization between disciplines.

Having defined the aim of linguistics as the synchronic study of language, Saussure focused on the system, which he described as made up of linguistic signs. As explained in Chapter 3, in Saussure's view, the linguistic sign is the association of a signifier (a form) and a signified (a meaning). The relationship between the two is just as arbitrary as the link between word and thing.

But how does the system, which combines these signs, work? It works on difference and opposition, according to Saussure. This is another crucial concept for the understanding of his theory of language and structuralism in general. It is the idea that, within a given system, everything is related to everything else. The elements that constitute the system are not defined by what they are, but by what they are not. Differences are more important than similarities. In English, for example, the signifiers *feet* and *fit* are not to be confused (they are the same except for the crucial *ee/i* difference in sound); the signifieds *sheep* and *mutton* are not to be confused either (they refer to the same animal, but in the first instance it is alive, and in the other it is dead). In cases of confusion, the whole system is upset, and communication becomes difficult. This is why, for example, it may be hard to communicate in English with French people who do not distinguish between the *ee* and *i* sounds or do not differentiate between *mutton* and *sheep*. If the French do not usually make such differences, it is because in their own language, these differences are not 'pertinent'; they have no bearing on the French language system. The implications of this are crucial for the understanding of the language system and all systems. On the one hand, difference constitutes the system and enables it to work; on the other hand, it is the system that defines which type of differences are relevant, or not, to its workings. This emphasis on interrelations between the elements within the system, and interdependency between the system and its constitutive elements was a breakthrough.

THE ORIGINS OF STRUCTURALISM

Structuralism was born out of the bold attempt, by French social anthropologist Claude Lévi-Strauss, to use linguistics as a model for the study of kinship and myth in pre-industrial societies. For Lévi-Strauss, communication formed the basis of human communities. He therefore suggested, in the late 1940s, that anthropology must learn and develop its methodology from modern forms of linguistics derived from Ferdinand de Saussure's *Course in General Linguistics*. He went on to describe, in minute detail, social relations within Indian tribal societies in South America, to establish the general, unconscious, patterns on which these human communities were organized. As Claude Lévi-Strauss's work became known outside the field of anthropology, many of his contemporaries followed his example. Thus, Saussurean linguistics became the 'pilot' science that lead the way in the social sciences and humanities.

> **The Structuralist Movement**
>
> The work done in the mid-1940s by the French anthropologist Claude Lévi-Strauss who introduced structuralist principles to a wide audience. His example was soon followed in France by Jacques Lacan (psychoanalysis), Roland Barthes (literature and language), Louis Althusser (Marxist philosophy) and many others.
>
> Structural analysis examines behaviour, institutions, language and cultural phenomena in terms of underlying networks of relationships within a system. In themselves, the elements that constitute these networks are meaningless: they are made meaningful by their role and place within the system.
>
> The structuralists question the view that we are what we make of ourselves. For them, the social existence, mental life, and cultural experiences of the individual are shaped by socio-economic, psychological and linguistic structures which the individual has not created and does not control. This is why structuralism has been regarded as 'anti-humanistic'.

Barthes was impressed by the way Saussure's theory could be adapted to account for other systems and by Lévi-Strauss's achievement in this respect. In Chapter 3 we saw how Barthes, having collected in the form of newspaper articles the contemporary myths that make up his *Mythologies*, turned to linguistics to find how mythical meaning was made possible. Although the theoretical model put forward in 'Myth Today' was not altogether satisfactory and needed the refinements proposed in *Elements of Semiology*, it was a significant first step towards a science of signs based on a structuralist methodology. Similarly *On Racine*, with its emphasis on functions, represented one of Barthes's initial moves towards the study of literature as a system. The controversy with Picard only served to encourage a more radical approach and hasten Barthes along the way to a structuralist theory of literature. The view of literature as a system was not entirely new – there had been significant precedents in Russia and Eastern Europe – but these were quite unknown in France until Lévi-Strauss introduced them to his contemporaries.

The decisive influence on Lévi-Strauss himself, had been the Russian linguist Roman Jakobson (1896–1982), whom he had met in the US where both had emigrated to flee Nazism in the 1940s. Jakobson's influence was two-fold: he contributed to the development of structuralism both as an eminent linguist with a keen interest in literature and as a disseminator of ideas. In the late 1910s and 1920s (i.e. before and after the Soviet Revolution of 1917), Jakobson had been associated with a movement, now known as Russian Formalism, which applied concepts derived from Saussure to literary theory. In the late 1920s, when Soviet Russia entered the repressive Stalinist era, Jakobson moved to Czechoslovakia, where he became a leading member of the Prague School, which contributed to significant developments in Saussure's theory of language.

It was Jakobson who introduced Lévi-Strauss – and, through him, many others including Barthes – not only to Saussure and the Prague School of linguistics, but to the Russian Formalists. Although their work dated back to the 1920s, it had been largely ignored for several decades and was not available in translation. It only came to be fully appreciated and understood with the advent of structuralism. When finally translated into French in the mid-1960s, notably by two of Barthes's students, Julia Kristeva and Tzvetan Todorov, it proved important for the development of a structural approach to literature and narrative in particular.

THE FORMALIST APPROACH

The following brief outline of some of the tenets of **Russian Formalism** will show remarkable convergence between Barthes's ideas and those of the Russian school. The theories of the Russian school worked as a catalyst for Barthes. They helped him to develop and formalize his own approach and, consequently, he was able to revolutionize the study of literature.

Russian Formalism (approx. 1916–1935) The leading figures in the Russian Formalist movement were Roman Jakobson, Victor Shklovksy, Boris Eichenbaum, Boris Tomashevsky and Yury Tynyanovsaw. They saw literature as a special use of language and advo-cated a scientific approach towards the analysis of creative writing.

As Barthes himself would do much later, the Russian Formalists started by questioning the value of biographical, psychological, and sociological studies as keys to understanding literature. They considered literature to be, above all, about language and, therefore, used Saussure's theory of language as the basis for their work. By attempting to define clearly the subject matter of literature – a special use of language – the Formalists granted the study of literature the status of a science, based on a firm theoretical grounding and an accurate terminology. They viewed the work of literature as a system, a complex unity of component parts that must be studied in relation to each other. Their aim was first to analyse the structural laws organizing specific works and specific fields of literature, and then to relate them to other fields in order to set up a limited number of structural types. Eventually they wanted to relate literature to non-literary phenomena to find further laws, i.e. a 'system of systems'.

VLADIMIR PROPP'S ANALYSIS OF FOLK TALES

Among those closely associated with the Russian Formalists was a folklorist named Vladimir Propp (1895–1970) whose work *The Morphology of the Russian Folk Tale*, published in 1928, only became available in West European languages after the Second World War.

Barthes himself read it in the late 1950s, at the suggestion of Lévi-Strauss, in an English translation.

In his study of Russian folk tales, Propp isolated two types of components: 'roles' which may be fulfilled by a variety of characters, and 'functions' which make up the plot. Working on a corpus of 100 tales, he identified seven standard roles and 31 standard types of actions which have a significant impact on the development of the story as a whole. A single type of action can fulfil different functions and a single function can be fulfilled by different actions. For example, the hero being turned into an animal or acquiring a new social status by building a huge castle can be, in different tales, instances of one and the same function: 'transfiguration' (i.e. the hero takes on a new appearance). Conversely, building a huge castle may be an instance of 'transfiguration' in one tale and a 'difficult task' in another. Although not all the functions appeared in every tale, when they did, they tended to appear in the same order. By showing that certain underlying narrative structures remain constant, despite the apparently endless diversity of forms and content, Propp's work made it possible, as Barthes explained later, to 'apply semiology with some rigour to a literary object, narrative'.

THE STRUCTURAL ANALYSIS OF NARRATIVES

Barthes's 'Introduction to the Structural Analysis of Narratives' published in 1966 proved to be yet another seminal work. Taking into account Propp's analyses, the latest developments in structural linguistics and the work of his friend A.J. Greimas, Barthes offered both a synthesis of what the study of narratives had revealed so far and a programme outlining what remained to be theorized.

Barthes saw literature as a privileged vehicle of narrative, hence most of his examples came from novels, notably James Bond novels. This does not mean that narrative is only to be found in literature. As Barthes pointed out in the opening paragraph of his article, narrative is an international, transhistorical and transcultural phenomenon. It can be found everywhere: in myth, epic, history, drama, mime, painting, stained-glass windows, cinema, comics, news items and so on. Because it is so wide ranging in its manifestations, narrative seemed a most appropriate object of study for the structuralists. Faced with such a multifaceted cultural phenomenon, Barthes compared himself to Saussure, trying to account for innumerable 'utterances' by describing the 'language' that enable them to be produced. He therefore suggested that narratology – the study of narrative – use linguistics as a model and proceed scientifically – by deduction. This involved the following: drawing a hypothetical model of description from a sample; comparing different types of narrative to this model and noting the similarities and differences; and then, finally, modifying the model to account for these variations.

At this stage in his thinking, Barthes thought that narrative could be approached from three distinct but interconnected points of view: functions, actions and narration.

* **Function**. The analysis of narrative as a system first required that it was divided up into its smallest constitutive elements. These elements or narrative units would be defined by their function and their import for the narrative. Some episodes could be described as hinge-points – decisive moments in the plot. Trivial incidents, which were merely used to 'fill in' the narrative space between the hinge functions, were seen as serving a variety of purposes – to delay the action, to provide indications of time and/or space, to create an atmosphere. A systematic analysis of this kind, Barthes suggested, would help to understand how different units can be strung together and, eventually, lead to a grammar of narrative.

* **Action**. Barthes used the notion of action to supersede that of character. Characters were defined, not as 'beings' (what they are), but as participants (what they do) since it is their role in the action described by the narrative that is of importance. Approaching characters from this perspective dismissed any notion of

psychology: characters were seen first and foremost as artificial 'constructs'; as characters, they might be more or less convincing, but that was no more than a technical problem.

❋ **Narration**. The term was used by Barthes to refer to the act of telling a story, and it covers a whole range of issues which, at the time, had barely started to be discussed, notably: 'Who is telling the story?', 'Who is telling the story to whom?', 'What are the different ways of telling a story?', and ultimately 'What are the connections between the answers to all these questions?'.

While *Elements of Semiology* (1965) had provided a blueprint for the semiological analysis of a wide range of systems of signs, Barthes's 'Introduction to the Structural Analysis of Narratives' (1966) provided a general framework for the study of narratives, whatever form they might take – literature, cinema, painting – as well as a narratological programme that would occupy scholars for several decades.

❋ ❋ ❋ SUMMARY ❋ ❋ ❋

● Barthes's approach to literature was inextricably linked to the French structuralist movement of the 1950s and 1960s.

● Structuralism appeared in different forms: it included the work of anthropologists, sociologists, philosophers and psychoanalysts, as well as linguists and literary critics. Their methods and goals, however, were comparable.

● The structuralists introduced the principles of Saussure's linguistics in the social sciences and humanities. They viewed society and culture as systems of interrelated signs whereby each sign is made meaningful by its place within the system.

● Barthes was also influenced by Vladimir Propp's analysis of Russian folk tales (1928) and, more generally, by the Russian Formalists (1916–1935) who suggested that literature is above all concerned with language.

● Barthes's Introduction to the Structural Analysis of Narratives' (1966) provided a blueprint for the systematic study of narratives: narratology.

Reader, writer and text 6

Predictably, Barthes's next major publication, *S/Z* (1970), was an ambitious and sustained analysis of narrative. It focused on *Sarrasine*, a novella by the French nineteenth-century writer, Honoré de Balzac.

In scope, *S/Z* was similar to *The Fashion System*. However, unlike *The Fashion System*, which was both an extension of and a logical conclusion to *Elements of Semiology*, *S/Z* questioned and abandoned some of the premises of the 'Introduction to the Structural Analysis of Narratives'. By deviating on key issues from the programme outlined four years previously, *S/Z* seemed to mark yet another new departure for Barthes and inaugurated what became known as Barthes's post-structuralist period.

Sarrasine

Honoré de Balzac's novella told a story – that of a sculptor named Sarrasine – within a story – that of a young man in love who hopes that the telling of Sarrasine's story to his beloved will earn him her favours. The sculptor's story is also about love: having, by chance, heard La Zambinella sing on stage, he falls madly in love and abducts the Italian singer, only to find out that La Zambinella is a castrato. Distraught at being so cruelly deceived, Sarrasine threatens La Zambinella and, as a result, is murdered on the orders of the singer's protector.

One of the characteristics of Balzac's novella is that both the reader and Sarrasine are victims of deception. Just as La Zambinella plays upon the expectations and false assumptions of the sculptor, the narrative plays upon those of the reader.

S/Z

The title of Barthes's book combines the S of SarraSine with the Z of La Zambinella. In French, there is a close relationship between S and Z: in the middle of a word S is pronounced the same as Z, and the two letters are nearly mirror images of each other. Barthes suggests that Sarrasine (the sculptor) is contemplating in La Zambinella (the castrato) his own reflection.

LEXIAS AND CODES

In true structuralist fashion, Barthes proceeds by breaking down Balzac's novella into its constitutive elements. These elements are reading units whose length is determined pragmatically during the course of a line-by-line discussion of Balzac's novella. The text is thus divided up into 561 successive fragments or 'lexias', of varying lengths. Lexia no. 1, for example, is composed of a single word – the title – while no. 21 is 18 lines long.

Each lexia is a portion of text that is recognized as having a different meaning or effect from the neighbouring units. Its significance is dependent on the **reader**'s ability to recognize it as a block of meaning and interpret it according to five **codes**, identified as being essential to the understanding of a narrative like *Sarrasine*. These codes, which enable the reader to follow and make sense of the narrative, are based on what might be called the 'already' of culture: everything that has already been read, heard, and generally experienced prior to this reading.

KEYWORDS

Reader: the embodiment of the codes that permit reading.

Codes: discursive and literary conventions and habits of reading.

THE FIVE CODES

The hermeneutic code – whose name is derived from the Greek verb meaning 'to interpret'. The function of the hermeneutic code is to create uncertainty and foster curiosity. It is the code on which detective stories and thrillers depend for suspense, but which is present in all narratives. In *Sarrasine*, the enigma begins with the title, which elicits the question: 'Who or what is *Sarrasine*?', and is answered at a later stage in the novella, with the biography of the sculptor. By then, obviously, many other new questions have been raised by the text.

The hermeneutic code generates various strategies and devices aimed at capturing and maintaining the reader's interests: **snares, equivocations, partial answers, suspended answers** and **jamming**. The snare is an evasion of the truth, meant to mislead the reader: the descriptions of La Zambinella's behaviour, for instance, suggest femininity and imply that the singer is a woman. Equivocation mingles truth and snare, and therefore helps to thicken the enigma: for example, the correct answer to the enigmatic behaviour of one of the characters is provided among a list of other equally credible explanations or the answer is both true and false depending on how it is interpreted. The partial answer exacerbates the desire for a complete and satisfying explanation. The suspended answer is when the answer to a question raised in the narrative appears to be imminent, and yet is postponed: for instance, the beginning of an explanation is overheard but not the end because the characters lower their voices and move away from the narrator. Jamming is when the enigma is declared insoluble: traditional narratives tend to provide plausible answers, but there are instances in which there is no ultimate 'truth' and the narrative thread is left hanging. For example, in *Adventures of Arthur Gordon Pym* by Edgar Allan Poe, the central narrative stops in mid-sentence and is followed by a chapter entitled 'Conjectures'.

The proairetic code – whose name is derived from the Greek word used by Aristotle to describe how the result of actions can be rationally determined. The proairetic code determines and helps the reader identify the various actions which, arranged logically according to the conventions of narrative discourse, constitute a coherent story line. The actions that provide the backbone of *Sarrasine* are listed by Barthes at the end of *S/Z*. The career of the sculptor, for instance, is constituted by six actions, distributed sequentially among different lexias: Go to Paris (lexia no. 167), Find a teacher (no. 169), Leave this teacher (no. 181), Win an award (no. 182), Be reviewed positively (no. 184), Leave for Italy (no. 185).

The semic code – whose name is derived from *sema*, the Greek word for sign, and is related to 'sememe', the linguistic term for a basic unit of meaning. The semic code relies on connotation. It is notably the code that enables the reader to take in various details relating to the protagonists of the story and to interpret and combine them to gradually build up an overall view of the character. In *Sarrasine*, for example, the passage describing the sculptor as a youth playing with his chums, yields two different kinds of connotations: the first one is excess and violence, because of the unusual ardour Sarrasine puts into the games and their often bloody outcome; the other is femininity because whenever he finds himself in the weaker position Sarrasine bites his opponents, a behaviour which, Barthes suggests, accords with the stereotypic view of women. Each character is therefore constructed from all the connotations that are gathered here and there in the course of reading. Sarrasine, for instance, is an ambiguous character, destined to a violent end. Obviously these connotations depend on cultural associations and ideology; the traits that are interpreted as relevant to the make up of the characters are those which correspond to what we implicitly consider to be credible behaviour.

The symbolic code – whose name is derived from the Greek word meaning 'mark', 'token', 'outward sign'. The symbolic code is the way in which connotations fall into established, contrasted categories, such as cold versus hot, light versus dark, life versus death, good versus evil. In the example above, Sarrasine's behaviour during fights can be interpreted in terms of the opposition between male and female symbolism. Indeed *Sarrasine*, as a whole, can be read along these lines.

The referential code is closely related to the semic code, because connotations are often the product of ideology: what 'everybody knows', 'what goes without saying' – as Barthes used to say in *Mythologies*. This code includes everything that does not contradict current opinion and is, therefore, accepted as natural. It also gives the narrative the appearance of truth or reality, its 'verisimilitude'. In this sense, it has nothing to do with what is true or possible, but is about what people believe to be true or possible at a particular time. For instance, the impulsive behaviour of the sculptor in *Sarrasine* accords with the romantic notion of the artist, while the way La Zambinella teases the sculptor corresponds to nineteenth-century stereotypes of womanhood.

The **referential code** is slightly different from what Barthes calls 'reality effects' which also contribute to verisimilitude. Reality effects are those inessential details which have no bearing on the development of the narrative and, as such, are meaningless: for example, a ladle lying in a kitchen sink. They have no connotation other than 'this is reality'.

CODES, VOICES, THREADS

In *S/Z*, Barthes uses several terms concurrently to explain how Balzac's novella, and narratives in general, work: 'codes', 'voices', and 'strands' or 'threads'. These terms, which are at times, almost interchangeable, highlight different facets of the process that Barthes describes and the complexity of the object of his enquiries.

The term 'code' emphasizes that the comprehension of narrative is based on an existing set of *cultural* assumptions and expectations.

'Voices' emphasizes the *verbal* nature of these cultural assumptions and expectations, since our vision and experience of the world is, in Barthes's view (see Chapter 3) mediated by language. It also enables Barthes to explain the way in which the five codes work concurrently: he compares the literary text to a piece of polyphonic music, in which several codes or 'voices' can be heard together.

Barthes also uses textile metaphors. Like a woven fabric (the original meaning of the Latin word *textus*), a braid or a piece of embroidery, the text is a complex system of intersections in which all elements are related to one another. The terms 'strands' and 'threads' are used interchangeably to refer to the way the five codes run together and cross one another, the object of the analysis being to disentangle them. They also emphasize a view of the text as surface; the text has no depth. It is a surface composed of signifiers: through reading, various meaningful patterns emerge but Barthes's analysis does not emphasize any one of them at the expense of the others.

FROM STRUCTURAL ANALYSIS TO TEXTUAL ANALYSIS

Later, commenting on the evolution of his work, Barthes said that *S/Z* was more of a 'textual analysis' than a structural analysis. By that he meant that *S/Z* is already underpinned by the theory of the 'Text', which will become central to some of his subsequent writings (see Chapter 7).

In the opening pages of *S/Z*, Barthes affirms that the structuralist dream of finding the unique structure that would account for all narratives is, ultimately, unsatisfactory. If it were possible to draw up an all-encompassing narrative structure that could be applied to all texts, then any one of them would be equal to any other. At this stage in his thinking Barthes finds that this approach, which he had advocated earlier, is too reductive. Instead of placing the emphasis on the conformity of the text to a hypothetical model and thus locking it into a fixed structure, the analysis of narrative should, Barthes now suggests, highlight its 'difference'. The term 'difference' does not refer to what traditional criticism might call 'originality', since texts are based on known cultural codes. It means that each narrative is structured by the particular encounter and interplay between these shared cultural codes.

From this perspective, the text is no longer viewed as a construct – a finished product – but as an open-ended process, something that is being constructed through reading. Contrary to historical analysis which aims at finding out *where* the text comes from, and structural analysis which looks at *how* it is made, the textual analysis practised by Barthes in *S/Z* focuses on the reader's role in producing meaning and on the ways literary works achieve their effects by complying with or resisting readers' expectations. He achieves this, however, without proposing a closed and definite interpretation of the novella. He simply unlocks the text, disentangles its constitutive strands, and allows it to expand along coded avenues of meaning.

In that sense, *S/Z* is already part of what will be known as Barthes's post-structuralist period. Post-structuralism, however, must be understood not as a reaction against structuralism but as a gradual shift of emphasis.

FROM TEXT TO INTERTEXT

In *S/Z*, the notion of codes, or voices, is related to the key concept of **intertextuality**. The term intertextuality, first appeared as the translation into French of the concept of 'dialogism' created by Mikhail Bakhtin. Mikhail Bakhtin (1895–1975) was a Russian philosopher and literary theorist, who wrote a critique of Saussure's theories and how they were applied to literature by the Russian Formalists in the

> **KEYWORD**
>
> Intertextuality: the text viewed as a tissue of anonymous formulae, conscious and unconscious quotations, and fragments of existing texts disseminated through culture.

late 1920s. Bakhtin's work was unknown in France until the 1960s, when Julia Kristeva, one of Barthes's former students, translated his work into French. Kristeva, who became a prominent member of the literary group known as the *Tel Quel*, introduced Barthes to Bakhtin's work and promoted the notion of intertextuality at a time when the limitations of the structuralist approach were beginning to be felt.

The idea is that, just as language is acquired ready-made, discourse (that is to say the way we talk about things) is also acquired ready-made. For example, at the most basic level, when we tell or hear a story, we know intuitively how to tell it or interpret it because we have read or heard stories before. Thus Barthes points out that the episode of the abduction of La Zambinella in *Sarrasine* refers back to every other story of abduction ever told or written before. Every text is seen as a mosaic of conscious or unconscious quotations: it takes up formulae embedded in language and repeats, transforms and combines all kinds of discourses widely disseminated through language and culture. This is quite different from the traditional notion of 'influence', which assigns the origin of discourse to a particular recognizable source. Here the source is everywhere: it is everything that has been read, seen, heard and generally experienced. All experience being, in Barthes's view, mediated by language, the world – reality – is a text; that is to say the sum total of what has been and can be, said about it.

FROM AUTHOR TO READER

This notion of the text as intertext further undermines the idea of literature as an imitation of reality and as a means of expression (which Barthes had questioned earlier, see Chapter 4). The structuralist approach had enabled Barthes to shift the focus away from authors as sources of meaning, to the systems of signs that made meaning possible. Now, with *S/Z*, the emphasis is placed on the role of the reader who, as the embodiment of the conventions that permit reading, is the dynamic agent of meaning. Hence the title of Barthes's now famous article entitled 'The Death of the Author', which states that the birth of the reader marks the death of the author.

READERLY/WRITERLY

In the opening pages of *S/Z*, Barthes briefly distinguishes between the **readerly** text and the **writerly** text.

He cites *Sarrasine* as an example of readerly text because it is a traditional narrative based on stylistic clarity, conventional realism and linear development – it has a beginning and an end. While playing with the expectations of the reader, it never challenges or disrupts them

KEYWORDS

Readerly: follows and plays on established codes and conventions, allowing the reader to read passively.

Writerly: breaks away from established codes and conventions, and thus requires the reader to take an active – i.e. writing – role.

radically. It is a classical text, i.e. a text that finds its place and its *raison d'être* in existing codes and conventions.

The writerly text, on the other hand, does not exist as such and can only be glimpsed in existing texts. Because no existing system, code or convention can account for it, such a text can be written but not read, thus abolishing the distinction between writer and reader. This is why Barthes regarded the writerly text as an 'ideal' kind of text. Eventually, the concept of the 'writerly text' came to refer to a text that encourages the active participation of the reader, while the readerly text promotes passivity.

Barthes saw *S/Z* as a turning point in his thinking, saying that the detailed analysis of Balzac's 30-page novella, over several months, had changed the way he perceived the text: as it changed under his very eyes, he arrived at a new theoretical position. Henceforth, Saussure's theories would cease to be the main point of reference and were replaced by the theory of the Text (see Chapter 7). If some of the concepts proposed by Barthes in *S/Z* are somewhat difficult to pin down, it is because they are not yet fully formed.

The view of the text as an intertwining of codes became, however, immensely influential. Barthes's method of analysis was widely adopted and adapted to account for other signifying practices. In areas such as the narrative analysis of film, for example, it is now part of established methodology. The distinction between readerly and writerly texts fired the imagination of many, finding new relevance with the advent of the World Wide Web (see Chapter 9).

* * * SUMMARY * * *

- In 1970, Barthes produced his most elaborate structural analysis to date, *S/Z*: a line-by-line discussion of a nineteenth-century French novella.

- This analysis contained the beginnings of a new approach to writing and reading which was to be pursued in the following years.

- Barthes now placed the emphasis not so much on how texts are made, as on how the reader makes sense of them.

- Barthes, at this stage, viewed the text as an intertext which derived its unity and meaning from the reader's previous readings and experiences.

- Barthes also introduced a distinction between readerly texts, which can be consumed passively, and writerly texts, which challenge our assumptions and require an active form of reading.

Pleasure, the body and the self
7

THE THEORY OF THE TEXT

In 1971, Barthes published a short essay entitled 'From Work to Text' followed, in 1973, by an encyclopaedic article devoted to the 'Theory of the Text'. In both, Barthes explains that the theory of the **Text**, which was initially developed by Julia Kristeva, was born out of the encounter between Marxism, Freudianism and structuralism.

The theory of the text borrows from Marxism notions such as 'process' and 'productivity'. These terms, which originally referred to the transformation of raw materials into a particular product, highlight the characteristics of the Text as intertext (see Chapter 6). They also serve to emphasize, not so much the idea of structure, as that of structuring, i.e. the active production of meaning, involving both the producer and the reader.

Under the influence of the psychoanalytical theories of Jacques Lacan, who claimed that the unconscious is structured like language, the theory of the Text also introduces the notion of the 'self'. The textual approach, however, is quite distinct from the traditional Freudian approach criticized previously by Barthes (see Chapter 4). The Text is not seen as the repository of an unconscious hidden meaning, which originates in the 'self' of the author and pre-exists the literary 'work'. On the contrary because, according to Lacan, the subject and the unconscious only exist in language – are constituted by language – the Text is part of the construction of the self.

Meaning is not a 'given'. It is an outcome: the result of all the systems, conscious and unconscious, that come into play through writing and reading. In this sense, the Text is not the book one holds in one's hand, that is to say a complete and finished product conveying intended and pre-existent meaning, but a dynamic, never-ending process. In this context,

KEYWORDS

Signification: denoted meaning (everyday communication).

Signifiance: connoted meaning (construction of the self in the text).

the notion of **signification** gives way to that of **signifiance**. Signification, Barthes explains, has to do with communication, with an emphasis on denotation and fixed signifieds. With signifiance, the emphasis is on the signifier and connotation. The signifier is no longer viewed in relation to a stable signified, but in relation to other signifiers. The connotations of any given signifier are constantly challenged and modified by that of other signifiers. As a result, meaning is forever in a state of flux, elusive and proliferating.

The 'I' of the writer, the product of 'signifiance', is an unstable self always in the making through the Text. As is the 'I' of the reader. Writing and reading become, if not interchangeable, at least activities that are never defined in isolation from one another: they are conceived, discussed and defined as part of the same process.

These are indeed complex and difficult concepts, although generally understood at the time, which Barthes only integrates loosely into his thinking and, as such, are beyond the scope of an introductory book. For Barthes, these ideas result in an increasingly marked delight in forms and an expressed wish to 'play' with language.

WRITING

In an interview published in 1971, Barthes regrets being always asked to write in the theoretical or critical vein, saying that he would prefer to pursue the writing experience of *Empire of Signs*, an off-beat book prompted by several shorts visits to Japan and published, like *S/Z*, in 1970. *Empire of Signs* was almost the antithesis of *Mythologies*.

As a Westerner who did not know the language, Barthes became highly aware of the surface of things and saw Japan as a place where the delicacy of the form is everything and the content nothing – a system of pure signifiers. In this fragmentary account of Japan, there is an imaginative and reflexive quality that foreshadows *Camera Lucida* (1980), and indeed Barthes later observed that *Empire of Signs* liberated him as a writer.

In the 1971 interview, Barthes also explains that *S/Z* is closer to the notion of the Text than his previous critical writings. It is not so much that stylistically it is well written – Barthes was always a great stylist – but that his use of language is not merely instrumental. Although *S/Z* is, conceptually, very close to the seminars he gave at the École Pratique des Hautes Études, Barthes says that it is fundamentally different. What he remembers most about writing the book is not the working out of ideas, but the pleasure he took in assembling his comments and digressions, that is to say in composing the book. He adds that the other reason why he liked to think of *S/Z* as a Text is that its publication provoked some of its readers into writing to him. Carrying on from where Barthes has left off, these readers would find new connotations in the lexias commented upon in *S/Z* and would discover new paths to explore. It was as if Barthes had, in his own modest way, succeeded in creating an endless process in which elusive meanings proliferate and readers become writers, a characteristic of the Text.

In this sense, *S/Z* brought Barthes one step closer to the ideal point where the theory of the Text is eventually subsumed by the practice of writing – where the Text ceases to exist as theory and only exists as writing.

THE PLEASURE OF THE TEXT

Although the notion of pleasure was only developed at length in *The Pleasure of the Text* published in 1973, it was already present in Barthes's previous writings and appears retrospectively as fundamental to his work. What drove him to read and write, he often said, was pleasure. For example, his love of neologisms, for which he was famous, stemmed as much from his scientific concerns – each new concept requiring a new word, to avoid confusion – as from his obvious delight in playing with words and creating new signifiers.

In *The Pleasure of the Text*, the idea of pleasure relates more particularly to the notion of the subject as a 'desiring' subject – largely popularized by Lacanian psychoanalysis at the time. Because the first – and unconscious – object of desire, the mother, is irredeemably lost, the subject is perpetually engaged in activities of substitution involving language. The prime function of language, and hence literature, is to signify this fundamental sense of loss. Therefore, desire is the force that drives reader and writer endlessly to go from signifier to signifier in search of fulfilment and pleasure.

From this perspective, pleasure and desire include erotic representations, but are not confined to them. This is why in Barthes's discussion of the work of the notorious Marquis de Sade (1749–1814), the adjective 'erotic' does not refer to the pornographic scenes described, but to the language deployed and the narrative grammar of such scenes. For Barthes, the true eroticism of Sade lies in the structure of his sentences and in the way these develop.

Obviously, this notion of pleasure corresponds to a highly sophisticated literary sensibility – what Barthes described in *Writing Degree Zero* as a 'sixth', purely literary, sense, interior to readers and writers. However, textual pleasure is also discussed in much lighter terms: Barthes talks, for example, of the pleasure one may take in skim reading, concentrating only on key events in the plot, or dipping into a book in order to savour particular passages. For him, there is no such thing as good or bad reading habits, although some may yield more pleasure than others, depending on the book. Reading every single word of an adventure novel might prove unendurably boring, and skim reading *Finnegans' Wake* in search of the plot a frustrating experience.

The only theoretical distinction Barthes introduces in *The Pleasure of the Text* is between plain **pleasure** (*plaisir*) and **ecstasy** or bliss (*jouissance*). Plain pleasure is when the reader is in control and feels comfortable with the text: the reader then simply consumes the text. Ecstasy arises, on the contrary, when the reader is destabilised and caught in the whirlwind of the text. There is a powerful element of danger in ecstasy: the reader is somehow consumed by the text. Barthes does not produce clear-cut definitions of pleasure and ecstasy in his book,

KEYWORDS

The body: holistic view of the self as distinctive and undivided.

Pleasure (*plaisir*): reading as a delightful form of consumption.

Ecstasy (*jouissance*): reading as a deeply disruptive and indescribable experience.

but instead keeps adding here and there new shades of meaning. As a result, the notion of ecstasy is largely open to interpretation, many commentators seeing a link between 'ecstasy' and the 'writerly' text. This is a long way from the scientific discourse on literature that Barthes originally promoted, and some of the notions he introduces are baffling at first reading. The **body** is one such concept.

THE BODY

In *The Pleasure of the Text*, Barthes explains that pleasure is 'when my body pursues its own ideas' and, somewhat more clearly, in a 1974 interview, that 'writing is the hand, and thus the body ... the subject with its ballast of desire and the unconscious'. This notion of the body thus negates conventional oppositions between body and soul, between body and mind. It is the intimate self, an indivisible and distinctive entity.

Barthes's notion of the body is also exemplified in two articles often quoted by commentators on both classical and popular music: 'Musica Practica' (1970) and 'The Grain of the Voice' (1972). In 'Musica Practica', Barthes explains that the same music may be minor when one listens to it, and tremendous when one plays it 'even badly', which implies that there is a form of understanding and knowledge that springs from physical involvement, from the body. In 'The Grain of the Voice', he suggests a new way of listening to and appreciating music based on attentiveness to the 'grain' of the singing voice or the music. The grain of the voice itself, is that which transcends traditional values and established codes: it is beyond the meaning of the words and the way they are set to music, beyond the clarity of elocution and the expressivity of the execution, even beyond the phrasing and the timbre of the voice. It has to do, however, with 'difference', as Barthes said in *S/Z* (see Chapter 6), and 'signifiance'. It is the 'body in the voice as it sings', a distinctive voluptuousness. It is when the work becomes Text.

This last article provides a good example of the kind of approach that Barthes was pursuing at the time, and how concepts developed in a particular field, may be transferred to others. From the 1970s onwards, the impact of Kristeva's theory of the Text was such that everything could be, and was, discussed in terms of the Text. For Barthes, however, text, pleasure and body refer primarily to writing.

BARTHES, WRITER

The notion of the body enabled Barthes to address the issue of the 'self' confidently, without returning to the concept of the 'author', which he had systematically questioned (see Chapters 4 and 5). This new confidence manifests itself in the increasingly personal style of writing he adopts from *The Pleasure of the Text* onwards.

Except for *Sollers, Writer* (1979), a collection of essays on Philippe Sollers – Barthes's friend of many years and the founder of the journal *Tel Quel*, then under attack – Barthes's subsequent writings are removed from critical or theoretical concerns. The verb 'to write' becomes truly, as Barthes once suggested, 'an intransitive verb', a verb without any direct object. Barthes simply writes, he writes for the pleasure of it. The critic and theoretician finally give way to the writer and this, in turn, leads to a blurring between criticism and imaginative writing.

Barthes never wrote a work of fiction in the usual sense of the word, however. Literature, under his leadership, had entered a modern phase that went far beyond the point when one could innocently write sequential narratives built around characters. Barthes, therefore, wrote 'works of language', that is to say works in which fiction appears indirectly, the true focus being language itself.

The first of these is *Roland Barthes by Roland Barthes* (1975), a book in which he is both the author and the subject matter. Its publication caused quite a stir given that he had always expressed reservations about biography. But this was not a conventional autobiography. The inside of the cover of the book is inscribed with a hand written sentence warning that 'it must all be considered as if spoken by a character in a novel'. The tone is gently self-deprecating and Barthes keeps switching between the first person ('I') and the third person ('he'), at times within the same sentence. Furthermore, there is no story as such. The only part of the book that resembles a narrative consists of a mini photo album showing Barthes's family and his early life. This album stops when Barthes becomes a writer because, as he points out 'the only biography is of an unproductive life' – in other words his work becomes his life. The second part of the book is a series of apparently unconnected fragments that testify to Barthes's productive life, i.e. writing under titles ranging from 'Active/Reactive' to the final 'Monster of Totality', and including many others such as: 'Proper Nouns', 'Friends', 'Eros and Theatre', 'A Memory Of Childhood', 'Migraines', 'Colour', 'The Divided Self', 'The Alphabet', 'Tactics/ Strategy' and 'The Weather'.

Barthes's next book, *A Lover's Discourse. Fragments* (1977) was equally surprising because of its subject – love – and the way it was tackled. It consisted of fragments of statements that lovers address to themselves as well as to the absent figure of their beloved. These annotated fragments were assembled under various entries: 'Absence', 'Adorable', 'Anxiety'… and arranged in strict alphabetical order, like a dictionary.

Both books created a sense of provocative novelty and their fragmentary style accorded with Barthes's notion of the modern text as essentially disruptive.

✴ ✴ ✴ *SUMMARY* ✴ ✴ ✴

● From the 1970s onwards, Barthes became linked to the post-structuralist theory of the Text – the synthesis of structuralism, Marxism and Freudianism.

● The post-structuralists viewed the Text not so much as a structure, but as a never-ending structuring process involving producer and reader.

● As his own view of the Text evolved, Barthes placed less emphasis on theory and stressed ideas of pleasure and imagination.

● Barthes's last works were removed from theoretical and critical concerns and he finally became a writer in his own right.

Barthes and photography

Barthes's last published book, *Camera Lucida* (1980) was subtitled *Reflections on Photography*. It was not the first time that Barthes wrote about photography, there had been several precedents, notably in *Mythologies*. *Camera Lucida* was, however, Barthes's most extended essay on the subject. It set out to define the essence of photography, by elucidating the reasons why some photographs – notably one picture of his mother who had died in 1977 – affected him deeply, while others did not.

CAMERA LUCIDA/CAMERA OBSCURA

The title *Camera Lucida* (Latin for 'light chamber') which refers to an optical device pre-dating photography, was paradoxical. Its opposite, *camera obscura* ('dark chamber') would have been more appropriate since the word 'camera' is the shortened form of *camera obscura*. Every kind of camera is a dark chamber or box into which the image of external objects is projected by means of a lens or other image-forming device. The *camera lucida*, on the other hand, is an instrument by which the rays of light from an object are reflected by a prism and produce an image on paper placed beneath the instrument: this image can then be traced with a pencil. The original cover of Barthes's *Reflections on Photography* showed a man using such a device to draw, one eye on his model and the other on his sheet of paper. Explaining his choice of title, Barthes says that it is a mistake to associate photography with the notion of darkness. He would rather associate it with light, since photography is, as he explains, an image revealed by light.

In fact, the whole book is paradoxical. It is at odds with Barthes's previous writings and yet in keeping with the general evolution of his thought. It is both a highly personal essay in the autobiographical vein, and simultaneously one which stimulated theoretical debate on the nature of photography.

Although photography cannot be said to have been one of Barthes's central concerns, his contribution to the subject was seminal because it brought to the foreground the question of the **specificity** of the medium, at a time when photography was coming into its own. Looking in some detail at the way Barthes tackles this subject affords the opportunity to measure how much his thought and his writing changed over time, as well as to understand the originality and the impact of his work.

> **KEYWORD**
>
> Specificity: the special determining qualities of something. Ascertaining the specificity of an object of study is the first necessary step to establishing it as a new discipline.

THE ISSUE OF SPECIFICITY

Mythologies bears witness to the increasing public awareness of photography and its enhanced status after the Second World War. Two of Barthes's essays, for example, are reviews of photographic exhibitions: the now famous international touring exhibition entitled 'The Family of Man'; and *Photo-chocs*, a display of press photographs designed to surprise or shock.

At this stage, Barthes is keenly aware of the increasingly important role of photographic images in everyday life, and he discusses photography mainly in relation to their subject matter. In this sense, the essays included in *Mythologies* reflect the dominant attitude to photography at the time. It is primarily seen as a tool in service to history, social documentation, fashion, science, advertising, rather than a medium in its own right.

Barthes's first major contribution to the study of photography as a medium was an article entitled 'The Photographic Message' (1961). This discussed photography in terms of denotation and connotation and went on to define the relationship between text and image in the Press. Most importantly, it stressed that the photograph is not 'simply a product or a channel but also an object endowed with a structural autonomy'. However, unlike in other fields, notably cinema, where

Barthes's early work immediately prompted a wealth of research, his articles on photography did not initiate a powerful semiological trend in the 1960s and 1970s. Susan Sontag's *On Photography*, was among the few exceptions. In fact, the analysis of photography per se only really flourished in the 1980s.

By the late 1970s, Barthes was still correct in pointing out that outmoded classifications remained the order of the day. Publications dealing with photography were usually technical manuals for the professional or the amateur, studies devoted to the history of the medium and its importance in society, or books concerned with particular genres (landscapes, portraits, nudes), significant trends (pictorialism, realism) or individual photographers. A single unifying theory dealing with the specific characteristics of photography was lacking. Then came *Camera Lucida*. It was a remarkable book in many respects. However, one of its important merits was to stimulate the debate on the specificity of photography, at a time when photography was thriving and there was a keenly felt need to establish a coherent theoretical framework in which to discuss it.

DENOTATION AND CONNOTATION IN THE PHOTOGRAPHIC MESSAGE

In 'The Photographic Message', Barthes made a bold statement, which he immediately qualified but did not retract: 'photography is a message without a code'. By that he meant that contrary to what happens with language, where the relation between the sign and its object is based on a conventional association of the two – the linguistic code that enables us, as we learn to speak, to name things – with photography there is no relay between the object and its image. Instead there is a direct, physical connection between the sign and its object: a photograph is the imprint on a light-sensitive surface of the luminous rays reflected by an object.

A photographic image does not describe reality, it does not tell us about it. A photograph reproduces reality mechanically, hence its immediacy – what Barthes calls its 'plenitude'. This is the reason why Barthes insisted that photography signifies first and foremost by denotation. The denoted meanings of a photograph are those elements that we recognize at the most basic of levels: a particular person, a particular smile, a particular place, a particular building.

Barthes was, nevertheless, quick to acknowledge that photography is not purely objective and that, in every photograph, there are also connotated meanings i.e. second-order meanings based on associations of ideas within a particular society and culture. These meanings are conveyed essentially by pose (gestures, attitudes, expressions), objects and setting, technical effects (lighting, exposure, colour, printing techniques, framing), aesthetic effects (whereby subject matter or composition evoke other art forms, such as painting) and syntax (photographs juxtaposed in order to form a sequence).

Examples of almost every type of connotation can easily be found in *Mythologies*, although at the time Barthes was not yet using the term 'connotation' to describe second-order meaning. A particular pose used by politicians – eyes half closed with a knowing gaze – is described as suggesting a mixture of social idealism and bourgeois pragmatism. In pictures of male actors, for instance, tobacco pipes, dogs or mantelpieces against which to lean, can suggest virility. In other pictures of actors and actresses, the soft lighting gives the face a dreamy, ethereal quality, which accentuates the extraordinary character of the figure. With 'The Family of Man', it is the syntax of the exhibition – the way the 503 photographs are grouped around subjects relevant to all cultures, such as love, children, and death – that promotes the notion of the universal and eternal nature of man, to which Barthes objects strongly.

Obviously, Barthes was speaking of analogue, as opposed to digital, photography. Although manipulations and distortions are easier in digital photography, trick effects are possible with traditional photography. Barthes saw trick photography, such as the removal and/or the addition of subject matter from an image, as connotation. He explained that, when unnoticed, trick effects are a form of connotation that passes off as denotation. Trick photography plays upon the fundamental characteristic of the medium, which Barthes would define in *Camera Lucida* as 'that-has-been', a belief that what is represented existed at one point in time and space.

STUDIUM AND PUNCTUM

In the same way that Barthes moved from the study of how literature makes meaning possible, to that of how the reader makes sense of the text, in *Camera Lucida* he placed the emphasis primarily on the viewer.

He used the terms **studium** and **punctum** to refer to two different, and sometimes concurrent, ways of being affected by a photograph: what distinguishes them is intensity. The *studium* is an *average* affect – originally in Latin *studium* did not mean 'study' but referred more specifically to a taste for something, a certain active interest. The

> **KEYWORDS**
>
> *Studium*: mild interest – to like.
>
> *Punctum*: intense interest – to love.

studium is an extremely wide field, which includes various forms of general, cultural, curiosity in photographs – a kind of enthusiastic but fundamentally distanced interest, a form of liking. By contrast, the *punctum* is an acute affect – in Latin, *punctum* means a sting, a cut, a puncture. The *punctum* is described by Barthes as an 'accident': something in a photograph that pricks the viewer, pierces his or her consciousness and is perceived as poignant. If the *studium* is similar to liking, then the *punctum* is comparable to love.

A large number of photographs are published every day. More often than not, they arouse interest for general, cultural reasons. They satisfy the curiosity of the viewer, provide information or give pleasure, as *studium*. Barthes takes the example of a photograph by William Klein entitled 'Mayday, Moscow. 1959'. He explains that, from it, he learned how the Russians dressed at the time. He notices such photographs because of his interest in the world at large, but he does not 'love' them.

However, sometimes it happens that one of the photographs he appreciates as *studium*, contains something – a detail – that strikes him like lightning: the *punctum*. In one photograph, it is the shoes of a woman in the picture, in another the bad teeth of one of several children portrayed. In the photograph representing a blind violinist led across the road by a child, the *punctum* is the dirt road itself whose texture gives him the 'certainty of being in Central Europe'. The *punctum* is not to be confused with shock: it is not the result of a deliberate attempt by the photographer to surprise. On the contrary, it is a detail that accidentally disturbs, arousing all sorts of feelings – sympathy, recognition, repellence – difficult to analyse but characterized by their intensity, their unexpected violence. The paradox is that the *punctum* is both in the photograph (the detail in question exists) and in the eyes of the beholder (the detail in question is perceived in a particularly acute fashion).

THE ESSENCE OF PHOTOGRAPHY

Camera Lucida consists of two parts, each divided into 24 sections. The first part is devoted to the difference between *studium* and *punctum*, while the second part focuses on a particular type of *punctum*.

At the beginning of Part I, Barthes relates an experience that was crucial for him. One day he chanced upon a photograph of Napoleon's youngest brother, Jerome, taken in 1852 and he realized, with amazement, that he was looking at eyes that had looked at the Emperor. Unfortunately no one seemed to share Barthes's amazement. Henceforth, besides his 'cultural' interest in photography, there remained at the back of Barthes's mind, the nagging desire to know what photography was 'in itself'.

At the beginning of Part II, Barthes relates another experience that took place 'one November evening' as he was going through photographs of his recently deceased mother. None of them seemed right, they only bore a partial likeness to her, except for one: a photograph of his mother as a child – a child he never knew – which did not look like her but which was, for him, a 'true' image of her. Overwhelmed by the 'truth' of this image, Barthes goes on to explore what is the nature of this particular *punctum* and comes to the conclusion that it is time itself: 'in front of the photograph of my mother, I tell myself that she is going to die'. By testifying that the person in the picture has existed, the photograph places the emphasis on life and provokes a reaction of 'there-she-is'. However, because the reality pictured is in the past, the photograph also implies that she is already dead. The testimony of the photograph bears not on what is represented, but on time. It is an image which, as Barthes explains, produces death while trying to preserve life. Hence Barthes's suggestion that photography is the pure representation of 'that-has-been' and, consequently, the representation of something or someone that is no longer.

The difference between his response to the picture of his mother and his reaction to Napoleon's youngest brother, comes from the fact that the heightened sense of recognition – 'there-she-is' or *punctum* – combines with the sense of time passing – 'that-has-been' or *studium*. The result is pure, unadulterated grief.

FROM SCIENCE TO PLEASURE, FROM PLEASURE TO GRIEF

In the first part of *Camera Lucida*, which focuses on the distinction between *studium* and *punctum*, Barthes reaffirms his dissatisfaction with systematic critical approaches, such as sociology, semiology or psychoanalysis, which he finds ultimately reductive. He chooses, instead, to be guided by the attraction that certain photographs exert over him. However, at the end of this first part, he comes to the conclusion that pleasure has been an imperfect guide, and that in order to find the true essence of photography he needs to 'descend deeper' into himself. It is only when he rediscovers his mother in the photograph of her as a child in a winter garden, that he feels he has finally discovered the true essence of photography and decides to 'derive' all photography from this one photograph.

The photograph itself is not reproduced in the book, unlike other photographs that Barthes comments upon. The reason Barthes gives for this is that, at best, the picture of his mother as a child would be of interest to his readers as *studium*, and that it could never act for them, as it does for him, as a 'wound'. The photograph is a pretext, literally. Only the intensely lyrical text can convey Barthes's sense of loss and grief.

Barthes is at pains to stress – and this is often overlooked – that he is not grieving for the loss of a mother figure, which we all have to face sooner or later, but that he is mourning the loss of a unique human being, a 'soul', without whom his life is 'without quality'.

AUTOBIOGRAPHY

Clearly, Barthes's approach in *Camera Lucida* is the antithesis of the deductive method used in semiology and 'The Photographic Message' in particular. Not only that, but the notions of universality, reality and truth which Barthes had so strenuously combated, dominate this autobiographical essay. And this is the final paradox. At a time when he seems to embrace what he has so systematically undermined, Barthes still manages to innovate, and in two specific areas: the fields of photography and autobiography. *Camera Lucida* takes what he had begun in his *Roland Barthes by Roland Barthes* (1975) a step further. He manages to breathe new life into the autobiographical genre, which all the innovative contemporary writers he had enthusiastically supported had carefully eschewed.

❋ ❋ ❋ SUMMARY ❋ ❋ ❋

● From *Mythologies* (1957) to *Camera Lucida* (1980), Barthes showed a lasting interest in photography.

● His last book, *Camera Lucida*, brought to the fore the question of the specificity of the medium, i.e. those features that differentiate photography from other signifying practices.

● Like any other message, a photograph can be analysed in terms of denotation (what the picture shows) and connotation (what the picture suggests).

● Another way of approaching photography is to examine how it affects the viewer: the viewer may be mildly interested (*studium*) or deeply touched (*punctum*).

● For Barthes, the *punctum*, a highly subjective feeling, was the key to understanding the essence of photography.

● The defining characteristic of photography, according to Barthes, is time: photography testifies that something or someone has existed while implying that they will die.

9 Barthes's legacy

When he was elected to the Collège de France in 1976, Barthes chose for himself the title of Professor of Literary Semiology. This confirmed that, in spite of his incursions into other fields, writing and literature had been, and remained, his main concern. Indeed, when he died in 1980, the general feeling was that his legacy laid primarily in the field of literature.

LITERATURE

Barthes's influence could be felt in the work of a whole generation of writers, both in and outside France. From the late 1950s onwards, French literature led the way in questioning established literary conventions, going through a process of drastic experimentation in the field of the novel known as *le nouveau roman* (the New Novel). This was followed by the attempt of the *Tel Quel* group, led by Philippe Sollers and Julia Kristeva, to create a revolutionary form of writing. Barthes supported them enthusiastically and contributed new ideas. However, the spate of difficult books that were published as a result, soon led to the disaffection of a large section of the reading public for 'serious' contemporary literature. Barthes's renewed emphasis on the value of pleasure found strong support and contributed to a change in the literary landscape: from the mid-1970s onwards, a number of highly innovative books with wide-ranging appeal were published. Meanwhile, in the wake of *Roland Barthes by Roland Barthes* (1975), autobiographical writing made a comeback, both as a genre and as an object worthy of study. Nevertheless, this return to more traditional concerns and forms was made with an acute awareness of the power of language and the codes that shaped all discourse, as acknowledged by John Fowles in the *French Lieutenant's Woman* as early as 1969.

On the critical and theoretical front, the considerable appeal of Barthes's structuralist project in France meant that narratology flourished in the 1970s, and that aspects of literary discourse were analysed systematically well into the 1980s. In Britain and America, the nature of Barthes's long-term influence was altogether different. Structuralism did not strike a particularly vibrant chord and, as far as literature was concerned, it was the post-structuralism of thinkers like Jacques Derrida and Michel Foucault that seem to have had the greatest influence. The main effect of Barthes's work was altogether simpler and more fundamental. On the one hand, it encouraged new ways of looking at literature, notably from ideological and sociological perspectives. On the other, it took literature off its pedestal as a higher form of culture and encouraged cultural studies. Literature became one signifying practice among many others whose specificity was gradually defined. This was the case with cinema, which provides a particularly apt example of Barthes's indirect and yet all-pervasive influence.

FILM STUDIES

Barthes's contribution to the development of film studies was no less important than his contribution to the study of photography, but it manifested itself indirectly. As we saw in Chapter 8, Barthes wrote little about cinema, and the semiology of film was originally developed by some of his former students.

Since the early days of cinema, much thought has been devoted to the moving image and filmmaking. However, it was only in the 1960s that film studies and film analysis started to develop as a specific field of enquiry and as an academic discipline. Since then, film studies have gone through three major phases. The first phase saw the emergence of a semiological approach to film: here, as in other fields, Saussure's structural linguistics provided the dominant model. During the next phase, post-structuralism became the preferred theoretical framework. Finally this was followed by a more pluralistic period when various movements, such as feminism, played an important role.

At each of these three stages, the influence of Barthes can be felt and, because of the importance of semiology in establishing film studies as a discipline, his legacy endures.

The 1950s and 1960s, in which the '*nouvelle vague*' flourished, was one of the most exciting periods in French cinema. Following Barthes's success in challenging the conventional views of culture, film gained further legitimacy as a cultural product worthy of serious attention. At the same time, the successful use of structural linguistics in the study of literature, myths and other cultural products encouraged the view that film might be approached as a system of signs consisting of 'signifiers' and 'signifeds', and discussed in terms of denotation and connotation. Eventually, Barthes's programme for the structural analysis of narratives and his approach to narrative codes, illustrated in *S/Z*, were also transferred from literature to film. What Barthes had done for literature, his followers did for film. The emphasis ceased to be on characters and plots: film was now seen primarily as an artefact. Innumerable analyses sought to capture the meaning of films by scrutinizing them shot by shot and identifying the codes at work within them. Although by the mid-1970s, film studies as a discipline was not drawing solely on Barthes-inspired theoretical models, it was still dominated by a mainly structural approach.

The next phase in film studies reflected the passage from structuralism to post-structuralism, and thus also mirrored to a certain extent, Barthes's own evolution. The merits of a 'scientific' approach to film were questioned and interest focused increasingly on the spectator. As a result, textual analysis gave way to the study of spectator positioning and the impact of texts on audiences. This shift of emphasis in the 1980s was also an answer to criticism coming from the field of cultural studies, where there was little interest in 'media specificity' and 'film language'. Instead, it was felt that all media, including cinema, should be embedded in a larger cultural and historical context. Textual analyses were criticized for being too reductive: they failed to take into account the fact that all artistic languages are fundamentally and inevitably social and historical. Thus the case against the various kinds of close analysis promoted by Barthes, was based on ideas remarkably similar to those expounded in *Writing Degree Zero* and *Mythologies*. It meant that one strand of Barthes's thought could be used to undermine an altogether different strand, developed at a different stage of his thinking.

In the current, more pluralistic phase of film studies where feminist theory, queer theory, minority discourse, post-colonial theory and new forms of historical analysis play a major role, Barthes's work continues to provide seminal references. Given his keen awareness of history, his interest in the way we are manipulated by cultural forms, as well as his overriding concern with meaning and the way we make sense of the world, this is hardly surprising.

HYPERTEXT THEORY

Another area in which Barthes has, more recently, proved influential is that of computer **hypertext**.

When Barthes died in 1980, personal computer technology was still in its infancy and the internet was just an American military data-transfer system. The widespread use of the personal computer as a medium for multimedia communication and interaction was but the dream of a handful of far-sighted American enthusiasts.

Yet, by the late 1980s, Barthes – along with some of his contemporaries such as Derrida and Foucault – was mentioned and quoted in the context of information technology, and especially in relation to hypertext.

KEYWORD

Hypertext: the term coined by Theodor Nelson in 1965 to refer to non-sequential writing. This radical new way of organizing information, led to the creation of computer games and encyclopaedic CD-ROMs, and then to internet websites. With the advent of the Word Wide Web in 1991, which greatly contributed to its development, hypertext became the most common internet application. Thus HTML stands for HyperText Markup Language and HTTP for HyperText Transfer Protocol.

Although literary theory and computer hypertext are unconnected areas of enquiry and have developed quite separately from one another, some hypertext specialists consider that Barthes's definition of the 'writerly' text in *S/Z* (see Chapter 6) precisely matched that of computer hypertext. They, therefore, see hypertext as the electronic embodiment of Barthes's 'ideal' text and they see Barthes's writings as offering a framework in which to discuss hypertext.

This is because hypertext is non-sequential writing. It is a text that branches and allows choices to the reader. It is basically a series of blocks of information (be it text, images or sound) connected by electronic links, which offer the reader different pathways and are best read interactively on a screen. Like Barthes's 'ideal' form of text, hypertext is, in principle, open-ended. It need not have a beginning and can be accessed from any number of entry points – none of which need be considered as the main gateway. It consists of an unlimited number of networks – none of which is superior to any other – and consequently favours an unlimited number of different readings and interpretations. It is a plural text that is always in the making. Far from being a passive consumer, the reader of both the writerly text and hypertext is an active, creative reader, who contributes to the making of the text. Hence the use of the word 'lexia', borrowed from *S/Z*, to refer to the individual blocks of information that make up hypertexts.

Having come to the conclusion that the writerly text, which could never be fully realized in print because of the limitations of book technology, has finally been made possible by the electronic medium, hypertext enthusiasts have felt that Barthes's theories might be applicable to hypertext. Accordingly, they have undertaken to put these theories to the test and to use them to theorize hypertext, most notably in the areas of textuality, narrative, and the roles or functions of readers and writers.

The newly found relevance of Barthes's work to the theory of the hypertext is not altogether surprising, given Barthes's predilection for writings consisting of fragments and his own peculiar way of working, which consisted in assembling notes and quotations written on index cards to see what connections might emerge. It was, in fact, Barthes's ability to make connections between different texts and approaches that enabled him to produce new lines of thinking.

It would be impossible to list all the contexts in which Barthes's name, and the concepts he helped to create, are mentioned today. Literature, film, cultural studies and hypertext theory provide, however, good examples of how diverse and far-reaching his influence has been. This is true both intellectually and geographically. Having spread from mainland Europe to the English-speaking world – notably, but not exclusively, through the semiotics of literature and film – Barthes's legacy has now started on another journey, from Britain and the US with cultural studies and hypertext theory, back to mainland Europe and onto Latin America.

The most important aspect of his legacy is that Barthes has taught successive generations that the way we think about the world is inseparable from the way we represent it. His relentless questioning of what we take for granted and his breaking down of artificial barriers, as well as his constant reassessment of the ideas and models he helped to shape, provide us with an enduring and stimulating intellectual model.

* * *SUMMARY* * *

• Barthes's influence is most visible today outside the field of literature, and it is particularly strong in the English-speaking world.

• Literature and literary criticism, like photography, offer examples of Barthes's direct influence. On the contrary, film studies have been indirectly – though no less deeply – influenced by Barthes.

• Computer hypertext is one of the many fields unrelated to Barthes's own areas of enquiry that has benefited from his insights.

10 Paradox: a way of thinking

Looking back on his career, Barthes explained that the notion of 'paradox' was fundamental to his development as a thinker. To free himself from *doxa* (the Greek word for received opinion or belief), he would posit a paradox (literally, a statement against received opinion). Then once this paradox became received opinion he would seek to formulate a new paradox. Thus, when the type of analysis Barthes proposed in *Mythologies* became the standard way of looking at cultural phenomena, he transformed the semiological approach into a fully-fledged science, able to rigorously account for a diverse range of signifying practices and, in doing so, opened up new fields of enquiry. Once this science of signs became what Barthes described as the 'often very grim' science of the semiologists, he turned away from this overly rational approach to stress notions of desire and pleasure in the text. When this new approach subsequently gave rise to what he regarded as 'endless prattle', Barthes shifted position once more. This time, he placed the emphasis on the writer, delving deeply into himself in his book on photography.

The later Barthes appeared to some of his contemporaries as having finally 'sold out' to dominant ideology. He seemed to be the very antithesis of the man who had so strongly opposed the traditionalists with his systematic approach to cultural practices and proclaimed the 'death of the author'. However, he never went back full circle. In his final opposition to any form of 'totalizing' theory and his rediscovery of the 'self', he kept renewing himself and the subjects he tackled. He never quite retraced his steps, hence the metaphor of the 'spiral' used by commentators to qualify his intellectual trajectory. Perhaps another way of looking at it would be to place Barthes's writings in their wider historical context and suggest that his evolution reflects, documents and, at times anticipates, that of European thought in the second half of the twentieth century, moving from Marxism to individualism.

Today Barthes appears, first and foremost, as someone who experimented with ideas, clearing the ground on which others would build. Not only did his writing succeed in questioning established beliefs in his preferred field of enquiry, literature and semiology, they also redirected thought in areas other than those to which they originally referred. Consequently Barthes has come to mean different things to different people, and his work provides key references for innumerable discussions in a wide range of fields from traditional literature to the avant-garde and cinema, from photography to advertising and feminism, and from music to fashion and the internet.

FURTHER READING

There are many books available both by and about Barthes. It might be useful to begin further reading with the following:

Books by Roland Barthes
Mythologies, Vintage, 1993
Empire of Signs, Hill and Wang, 1982
A Lover's Discourse, Penguin, 1990
Camera Lucida, Vintage, 1993

Selections of essays by Roland Barthes that are most representative of his work
A Roland Barthes Reader, introduced and edited by Susan Sontag, Vintage, 1993
Image-Music-Text, essays selected and translated by Stephen Heath, Fontana Press, 1987

Interviews with Barthes
The Grain of the Voice: Interviews 1962–1980, University of California Press, 1985

Books about Roland Barthes
Leak, Andrew, *Barthes: Mythologies*, Grant & Cutler, 1994
Culler, Jonathan, *Barthes: A Very Short Introduction*, Oxford University Press, 2002
Calvert, Louis-Jean *Roland Barthes*, Polity Press, 1996

Websites

Lectures on *Mythologies* by Tony McNeill, 1996
http://www.sunderland.ac.uk/~os0tmc/myth.htm

A piece of hypertext e-writing inspired by Barthes's autobiography by
Charlie Mansfield, 2001
http://www.ifrance.com/europapoesie/abc.htm

INDEX

HEIDEGGER – A BEGINNER'S GUIDE

Michael Watts

Heidegger – A Beginner's Guide introduces you to one of the most important and highly controversial philosophers of the twentieth century. Use this guide to help you unravel his revolutionary throughts on the nature of existence and the question of Being.

Michael Watts's informative text explores:

- Heidegger's background and the times he lived in
- the central ideas of Heidegger's work, in simple terms
- Heidegger's influence on ecology, art and literature
- the continuing importance of Heidegger to philosophy and contemporary thought.

NIETZSCHE – A BEGINNER'S GUIDE

Roy Jackson

Nietzsche – A Beginner's Guide introduces you to the life and work of one of the most widely read philosophers in the modern world. Use this introductory guide to help you unravel his philosophy and explore his work.

Roy Jackson's fascinating introduction:

- summarises Nietzsche's principal work
- explores how Nietzsche was influenced by various incidents in his life
- puts Nietzsche in philosophical and historical context
- explores Nietzsche's legacy.

WITTGENSTEIN –
A BEGINNER'S GUIDE

Sean Sheehan

Wittgenstein – A Beginner's Guide introduces you to the life
and work of this twentieth-century philosopher. Use this
introductory guide to help you unravel his philosophy and
explore his works.

Sean Sheehan's informative text explores:

- Wittgenstein's background and the times he
  lived in
- Wittgenstein's compelling personality and the
  course of his life
- the central ideas of Wittgenstein's work in simple
  terms
- Wittgenstein's continuing importance to
  philosophy and contemporary thought.

JUNG –
A BEGINNER'S GUIDE

Ruth Berry

Jung – A Beginner's Guide introduces you to the 'father of analytical psychology' and his work. No need to wrestle with difficult concepts as key ideas are presented in a clear and jargon-free way.

Ruth Berry's informative text explores:

- Jung's background and the times he lived in
- the development of Jungian analysis in simple terms
- dreams and their interpretation
- classic interpretations of popular myths and legends.